PEARL

THE AMAZING STORY OF FLORIDA PEARL

BY

JUSTIN DOYLE

JUSTIN DOYLE PUBLICATIONS

EDITOR

JUSTIN DOYLE

COVER -

PAULA WARD

DESIGN & LAYOUT

BERNADETTE MOLONEY

ISBN - 0 - 9549075 - 0 - 7

Copyright

Produced in Ireland by Justin Doyle Publications,
67 Anglesea Road, Ballsbridge, Dublin 4

For permission to reproduce articles and photographs in this book, the
author and publisher gratefully acknowledge journalists, Brian
O'Connor of The Irish Times; Ray Glennon of The Irish Independent;
Ronnie Bellew of The Sunday Independent; Michael Clower of The
Sunday Times; Pat Keane of The Irish Examiner; Jonathon Powell of the
Mail on Sunday and Alastair Down of The Racing Post.

Special thanks are due, in no small part, to photographers
Liam Healy, Hugh Routledge and Caroline Norris for the
great time and effort they afforded in order to file and
forward photos.

Acknowledgements

I am indebted to all concerned for their very kind
assistance in helping to put this book together.
Particular mention must be made to the following:

Trainer, Willie Mullins, spoke to Florida's owners on
my behalf and then put me in touch with them; the
O'Leary family then gave me permission to go ahead
and write the book while also gathering together a lot of
very important material for the book;

Tracey Gilmour, Florida's handler, put together the
Foreword; Michael Kennedy, former jockey turned
author; Tony and Mark in the Leinster Leader's printing
department; Sean MacAonghasa in the RTE Library and
especially to Bernadette Moloney for doing such a great
job in typesetting.

I also have to mention Martin Murphy and Michael
O'Rourke at Horse Racing Ireland; Toni Kelly at
O'Leary Insurances in Cork; Mirio Milla, Martin
Smethurst and John Randall at the Racing Post in
London and finally Brough Scott - as one of the finest
exponents of written and spoken word, his generous
contribution at the back of the book was the icing on the
cake.

Sincere thanks, and apologies, to anyone else who has
been inadvertently omitted.

Contents

Here's to the bundle of sentient nerves with the heart of a woman, the eye of a gazelle, the courage of a gladiator, and the proud obedience of a soldier - The Horse!

Anonymous

FOREWORD

It's that time of the year again when the days are shorter, the nights colder and in the normal course of events, Florida Pearl would be getting ready for his seasonal return at Down Royal or perhaps Punchestown.

Of course that is not happening this year and sadly, it will never happen again.

The Pearl has been formally retired but he is now having a great time out on the gallops each morning or doing a bit of dressage or show jumping. He still lives in his old box and yes, he still gets more attention than any other horse in the yard!

The year 2004 has been a real roller coaster of emotions for all of us here in the yard.

His comeback run and terrific win at Fairyhouse was a real tonic. That February day at Leopardstown after he won his fourth Hennessey when so many had relegated him - that was absolute magic. On that glorious day, all the stress, doubt and frustration of the previous year was made irrelevant.

His enthusiasm for racing and for life in general was contagious and this year the Gold Cup looked so possible. I was completely gutted when he injured himself and without him going over as part of our team, Cheltenham lost a bit of its gloss.

However, each morning as he head-butts me when I'm getting him his breakfast, he reminds me of all the good times and how great it is to have him around!

I can vividly recall a solidly frozen Kempton Park in 2001 with Christmas dinner at a petrol station deli and no jockey wanting to ride him in the King George.

But unlike me, Florida was relaxed, happy and bursting with good health. He seemed to enjoy every minute of that day and especially in the big race itself.

In the Martell Cup at Aintree, he just destroyed them and in Punchestown's Heineken Gold Cup, he was so brave and tough to fight back from a bad mistake close home.

Of course there's the record breaking four Hennessey's and also his brilliant victories at Cheltenham. However, apart from all the races he won, I'm especially proud of him for his tremendous second to the brilliant Looks Like Trouble. For a few moments in that 2000 Gold Cup, he real looked like winning.

As for the low points, they are few and far between and in any case, they're not worth remembering. Neither is the nagging drivel from those who insisted on devaluing his form or pointing out what they felt were his failings.

I have loved every moment of traveling with him throughout his career and meeting such legends as Richard Dunwoody and even the average punter who wanted to say hello and just enquired about the 'big horse'.

Florida Pearl would have been a Champion in any sphere. I am, and always will be, grateful that it was in mine.

Tracey Gilmour

CHAPTER 1

THE SEARCH FOR A STAR

Sitting behind his desk at Lough Mahon House, Blackrock, Archie O'Leary stares out at the pictures adorning the walls of his office. The framed photographs are mainly of a sporting theme. Photographs of his rugby days bygone and some horses he has owned, only serve to strengthen his resolve to find a decent racehorse.

No longer able to perform in sports he loved so dear, Archie now wants a bigger and better challenge. The novelty of simply having a runner wearing his colours at Cheltenham has long since worn off. He dearly wants to find a horse that will help to reawaken and reinvigorate the sporting and competitive nature still smouldering in his bones.

The very thought causes an upsurge in his body and he feels ignited with excitement at the prospect of the adventurous pursuit he is about to embark on.

At the outset, he knows the importance of teamwork. As a young sportsman, he played rugby for Cork Constitution, Munster and the pinnacle of his rugby career was winning three caps for Ireland in the second row position in 1952. In the tough world of sailing, his boat "Irish Mist" was part of the Irish team in the 1975 and 1977 Admiral's Cup. In the 1975 series Irish Mist led in the 700 mile Fastnet but unfortunately hit a calm 40 miles from the finishing line at Plymouth.

In his business dealings, Archie also had great success. After training in Dublin with Norwich Life, he set up his own Insurance Brokerage Company at No.87, South Mall right in the heart of Cork. The O'Leary Insurance Group now employs well over 150 people with offices in Cork and branches in Dublin and Galway. He achieved everything through teamwork and time. In setting out to find a racehorse with potential, he would apply those two principles to the task.

Mingling among friends at various race meetings, Archie let his intentions known. In doing so, the ball was set in motion for the team to play. The game was well and truly on when, on the advice of a friend, he went to meet with Willie Mullins. Mullins was one of Irelands leading up and coming young trainers and both had an immediate understanding. The young trainer agreed to help him look for a racehorse. Feelers and sensors were sent out. Everything was now in place and alarm bells were primed and ready.

High in the beautiful glens of Antrim, Patricia MacKean breeds horses at her Sweet Wall Stud. It is a modest run operation and more a labour of love than anything else. Like many other small family run businesses, she and her statt try very hard to make ends meet. At the end ot her working day, there is always the hope and dream that one day she will breed a racehorse that will go on to achieve success.

Unlike the vast almost industrial like studs at Coolmore and Moyglare, Patricia has just a few stallions for breeding. They only have ordinary pedigrees and had poor form on the racecourse so the odds on their producing a champion are very miniscule.

The biggest studs in Britain and Ireland have scores of stallions. Many of them won Classics and Grade 1 races and as a result, they do produce champions of the future.

One of Patricia's stallions is Florida Son. He has been covering (breeding with) mares now for over twenty years. His sire (father) was Busted who was a top class performer on the flat and he won several top races. But his mother was nothing special and so Florida Son only managed to win four ordinary races. As a stallion, he did at least produce sons and daughters but of those that made it to the track, nothing sparkled.

In the summer of 1991, Florida Son covered a mare named Ice Pearl. Her pedigree was equally unimpressive. She was an unraced daughter of the little known stallion, Flatbush. However, her mother Ice Blossom did have some quality in her blood.

She was related to a Cheltenham Chase winner named Iceman and she was also a half sister to the grandams of two regular runners at Cheltenham, Arctic Kinsman and Pearlyman.

In 1992, when Florida Son and Ice Pearl gave birth to a white faced and rather gangly male, it was just a case of another young foal delivered. Nothing born at Sweet Wall had ever shown anything on a racecourse before. As a result, there were few who expected that this new arrival would be any different from those that came before.

Tom Costello is a very well known horse dealer from County Clare. Time has proved that he has a very good eye and an excellent judgement of horses. He has spotted many high class horses and several Cheltenham Gold Cup winners were sold as youngsters out of his yard in Newmarket on Fergus.

A well worn route saw Tom travel from Clare to Meath in 1993 for the annual Tattersalls Horse Sales held at Fairyhouse. In the past he has come away from there with horses of the calibre of Midnight Court, The Thinker, Cool Ground and Imperial Call. All four won the Cheltenham Gold Cup so the excitement must run through Toms veins each year he returns to the Meath venue. As he watches the young horses parade through the ring, he knows he has what it takes to spot a champion.

When the yearling by Florida Son out of Ice Pearl was led around the ring, it caught Tom's eye. Whatever went through his mind, he did not buy. Mrs. MacKean had put a price of £3,500 on the horse and perhaps a quick look at the breeding put Tom off. Not surprisingly, because of the unfashionable breeding, there were no takers to meet that asking price.

It had been an uneventful and disappointing day. Patricia MacKean headed back up north through the narrow and hilly roads of Antrim with nothing to show for her long day. On the way back west to Clare, Tom was likewise a little perturbed. Unhappy with his lot, the eyes that had unearthed such equine gems of the past, were flashing an image around in his mind. Over the following days, the image continued to pester him and so he decided to have a second look at the bay gelding by Florida Son.

In pursuit of a potential champion, no road or journey will stand in the way of the Costellos. Although he was taking a big gamble in taking the long journey north, Tom trusted the courage of his convictions. The drive from Clare to Antrim paid off and he agreed a price with the MacKeans for the sale of the young horse. The final figure may have been a few quid more or less than the asking price but the deal was done. Such a deal, like many before, can also be a means to a huge profit and a few years later, Tom would reap the reward of his efforts and talents.

Three years after purchasing the horse, Tom and his family had worked hard in preparing him for his first race. At home, the horse had shown great zest for work and his appetite for food was such that he had developed into a powerful and muscular gelding. He was named Florida Pearl and his first race would be in a Point to Point just outside the Cork town of Fermoy at Lismore.

Like the quality horses that had passed through his yard, Tom knew this horse had potential and he awaited his first run with eager anticipation. The horse was showing him all the right early signs. He also knew that the horse possessed two of the most important ingredients - strength and speed. Through the pedigree, doubts remained about the stamina of the horse to race three miles and beyond. All would be revealed at Lismore.

Point to Points can be described as semi-professional racing and they are held in large fields. Unlike professional racing, there are no stands and no big betting facilities and the prize money on offer is very small. It is similar to Three Day Eventing or in human terms, Cross Country running. Nevertheless, they are covered by the National press and there are many shrewd judges present to view any talented horses and jockeys that may surface. Indeed, many horses and jockeys have come from these fields to reach the very top in the professional ranks.

Families like the Costello's, the Hogan's and the Bolgers are steeped in Point to Point racing. Their training, buying and selling of young horses means that they have a direct line to the top professional trainers and owners. With the news out that Willie Mullins was looking to pay a good price for a horse, it was only a matter of time before he and the Costello's met.

Willie Mullins had looked at several horses for Archie O'Leary but nothing really caught his eye. Then, on a cold February day in 1996, he went to the Costello's yard to look over several of their horses. The young Florida Pearl was actually owned by Tom's son, John. But he stood out head and shoulders above the rest and Mullins was smitten. To this day, Willie Mullins maintains that he has never seen such a horse. It was his sheer size and scope, the length of his stride and the muscle mass in his hind quarters that so impressed him.

He wanted to buy the horse there and then but John Costello would not sell. The horse was to run at Lismore the following week and shrewd as they were, they knew that if he impressed there, they would get a lot more money. It was a big gamble to take. Mullins would have paid perhaps £25,000 which was over six times what they bought him for. On the other hand if Florida Pearl flopped at Lismore, then in all likelihood Mullins would look elsewhere.

On Sunday, 3rd March 1996, Florida Pearl lined up for his first race. The sunny spring day meant that the event at Lismore was well attended. Florida Pearl would run in the Lismore Hotel 4year old Maiden which was the second of a seven race programme. The race was over a distance of three miles and the standard rate prize fund at the time was £400.

Tony Costello would ride and he wore the Clare colours of yellow with a blue stripe and blue epaulets. However, they were not the race favourites. That mantle was bestowed upon a horse of Tom Nagles, namely Perky Lad.

This horse was actually the subject of a huge gamble and a lot of big bets were laid on him that day. If that on course gamble came off, then the off course gamble taken by John Costello in not selling to Willie Mullins, would more than likely fail.

Nine runners lined up at the start. The hot favourite, Perky Lad, who had won two of his previous four races, went off in front and set a scorching pace. If that was to prove one thing, then it would show if Florida Pearl had the stamina to last the trip.

Coming to the second last fence, the favourite was still out in front and showing no signs of stopping. He had burnt off all bar two other horses and Florida Pearl was running six lengths behind in second. But in a sudden burst of acceleration, Florida Pearl responded to Tony Costello's urgings and he swept past the leader to win very impressively by 3 lengths.

He had more than answered all questions and now the Costello's knew they had a very special racehorse on their hands. More than that, they knew they had an unpolished and valuable gem. Their gamble had well and truly paid off and they could now sell him to the highest bidder. Willie Mullins was also very excited and he immediately notified Archie O'Leary telling him that he had finally found him a real racehorse.

Willie and Archie knew that they had to act fast. The press would report that win next day and there would be rave reviews relayed from Lismore by many other parties. To beat a hot favourite and experienced horse so easily, and in your very first race, was some feat. A couple of days later, both men travelled to Clare to begin their negotiations.

John Costello and his father Tom drove a very hard bargain. Finally Archie and Tom Costello had a private conversation during which Tom Costello stated that he had been offered £50,000 but owed Willie Mullins a favour and for that reason was not proceeding with his offer.

Willie Mullins confirmed privately to Archie O'Leary that Tom Costello was "for real" and the deal was done at a cost of £50,000 less some luck money. By some way, it was the most expensive horse Archie had ever bought and at the time, it was also the most expensive racehorse Willie Mullins had ever handled.

Valuations had spiralled since the horse's original price tag and even then the bidding was not over. Archie did not disclose to his family what he had paid in case they would be shell shocked. Instead he stated that the horse was expensive and he informed Violet that half of the horse was hers as a birthday gift. Everybody seemed happy at this outcome.

As a matter of interest, in that Point to Point race, the horse that finished six lengths behind Florida Pearl in 3rd place was ridden by a young Noel Fehily. In a race full of talent, Noel would later go on to become one of the top professional jockeys in England and he is now stable jockey to one of the top trainers over there, Charlie Mann.

The news about the Florida Pearl deal travelled fast, far and wide and as it did it raised enquiries from several others keen to get in on the act. Andrew Cohen, a millionaire owner in England and connected with the huge Betterware company, offered Archie O'Leary £120,000 for the horse. It was a very tempting offer especially since the sterling conversion to punts would add on a lot more money.

For a man accustomed to buying horses for up to a limit of around £10,000, this was an offer he had to think strongly about He had forked out a small fortune on a horse who had only won a small race.

What if the horse did not make it on the racecourse proper under National Hunt Rules? What if he picked up a career threatening injury? These, along with other questions, had to be seriously considered especially since the offer made would give Archie a near £100,000 profit on his outlay. It also meant that if he sold out, he could search again and buy two or three other racehorses.

In January 1998, in a Sunday Times feature by award winning sports journalist David Walsh, Archie explained why he turned down the offer:

"It was an awful lot more than I paid and I felt that I should discuss it with my family. I didn't want to sell but if they thought I should then maybe I would. But they said this wasn't about making money and anyway, how many beds can you sleep in, how many steaks can you eat? " They were all hooked on Florida Pearl. Some more buying approaches were made but Archie's final reply was "the house is for sale, the wife is for sale, I'm for sale but this horse is not for sale".

Following the sale, Florida Pearl was loaded onto Willie Mullins horsebox for the journey to his stables. He would now have to adjust to his new surroundings in County Carlow.

Everything was so much bigger. There were lots of horses, lots of stable boxes and lots of people. Perhaps the biggest change he would have felt was in the environment and terrain for after living near the Shannon and the salty winds sweeping in from the Atlantic, he was now stabled high above sea level at Bagnalstown in Carlow.

But for a horse reared in Ulster, brought up in Munster and a working career in Leinster awaiting him, getting used to his new surroundings would surely not be a problem.

After a month of getting to know his new stables, in mid April 1996, the serious business of working Florida Pearl began. Early morning runs on the all-weather gallops would help to build up his fitness levels, fine tune and tone his muscle mass and this would also help to increase his speed.

This would all be monitored along with his eating and drinking habits. He would also be assigned his own groom, his bedding changed each day and his box cleaned out. From now on, there would never be a dull moment in his new racing life

In return for all this, Florida Pearl was expected to deliver the success his big sales figure warranted. Early morning work on the gallops and his new stable routines were just the start of future plans mapped out by his new connections. Eight months later, he would be assigned his first real test and his first appearance on a racecourse.

His entry for a race at the big Leopardstown Christmas meeting was a measure of the high regard in which he was held. Before a large expectant public, and with RTE television cameras present, a good performance was essential. A poor performance would be so costly and expensive and as the months passed away and the big day neared, nerves and tension were understandably kicking in.

CHAPTER 2

GALLOPING TO GLORY

The huge crowds that turned up at Leopardstown on St. Stephens Day 1996, did not go home disappointed. Danoli, the Peoples Champion, was roared on to victory in the Denny Gold Medal Chase by seemingly everyone present in the 18,000 attendance. Word had also filtered through that, over at Kempton, the popular grey One Man had swept to victory in the King George.

The few unfortunates who had not backed either of those two horses to supplement their Christmas expenses, were in for another chance with the whispers going around about a 'dead cert' later in the day.

Prior to the Christmas Festival at the popular Dublin venue, many observers felt that Promalee would win the last race. However, the word spreading rapidly around the track was for a newcomer trained by Willie Mullins.

As the last race approached, Florida Pearl was lead out of his box and into the parade ring for the very first time in his life. What an unusual and alarming sight greeted him.

All around him, the place was packed full of people. The noise levels and the many different colours and smells must have been quite daunting and intimidating, even frightening. If it was, then he did not show it. He just swaggered around without any fuss and he took it all in his stride.

A few minutes later, a bell sounded. This was a sign for the jockeys to mount their horses. Willie Mullins then gave James Nash the leg up on Florida Pearl and both cantered down to the start for the Ballyfree Flat Race over 2 miles. The last race has always been known as the 'Bumper' as many punters, anxious to retrieve their losses, lump on in the hope of a last gasp windfall!

In the betting ring, and at the Tote outlets, there was a hive of activity. Almost everyone wanted to get on Florida Pearl as they deserted Aidan O'Brien's, Promalee. This resulted in Florida Pearl going off as the favourite. So much weight of expectation and so much money forced his opening price of 2/1 tumble to 6/4.

Twenty one other horses set off in the race. In such a big field, there is always concern that some mishap may occur. James Nash, a promising amateur jockey, settled Florida Pearl in mid-division and bided his time. So far, all was going well and the horse was running well.

Promalee, his big market rival, hit the front as they neared the entrance to the straight. But Nash came cruising through past beaten and tired horses into second place. The young jockey could not believe the powerful engine he had beneath him.

At the furlong marker, he eased Florida Pearl alongside Promalee. When he asked him for a big effort, the response was swift and decisive. The pair came home five lengths clear of the O'Brien horse with a further eight back to the third.

Those who put their punts on prepared to collect while connections were thrilled the horse had won and shown potential. But this was only the beginning. A point to point and a bumper did not really prove anything. There was a long way to go to prove his worth.

Afterwards, Willie Mullins stated that he had not really done much work with the horse. A lot of work remained and he announced that Florida Pearl would go straight to Cheltenham. He would run in the Champion Bumper without another prep race.

With just over ten weeks to that race, Mullins stepped up the horse's work rate considerably. He knew what it took to win the race as he had won it the previous year with Wither or Which. The race attracts all the best bumper horses from Britain and Ireland so he would have to have Florida Pearl as fit as a flea.

After seeing the way Florida Pearl was doing his best work at the finish of that bumper, something clicked in Willie's head. The bumper is run over two miles but he had also won his point to point over three miles in much the same way. He knew that the horse had stamina and he planned to use that to best advantage.

Horses running in the Cheltenham bumper are usually speedy, flat bred types. They would be very hard to beat but Mullins felt that most did not have the stamina Florida Pearl had. It would therefore be foolish to hold the horse up on the tails of the leaders this time.

If the speedy types got first run, then Florida Pearl would struggle. The plan was to burn the speed out of the rest by setting and sustaining a ferocious gallop.

Willie Mullins and his staff did their best in having Florida Pearl in perfect shape for his big race. After travelling to England by ferry, the horse was stabled near the racecourse. They had arrived in one piece and everything was now down to the horse.

On Wednesday 12th March, Florida Pearl would run in the last race at 5.40. The first race at 2pm heralded the arrival of a superstar. The brilliant Istabraq won for the first of four consecutive years at Cheltenham.

Three and a half hours later, it was the turn of Florida Pearl to take to the track. He opened up as 3/1favourite for the Weatherbys Champion Bumper. Ridden by the great Richard Dunwoody, he would face twenty four rivals all super fit and ready to run to their very best.

The chief threats were French Holly and Samuel Wilderspin. Then, as doubts surfaced about Florida Pearls ability to beat some of his rivals for speed, his price drifted. He went out to 6/1 as punters made Jim Old's Dawn Leader the 4/1 favourite.

In the event, the favourite was a spent force along way from the finish. After a furious pace was set, which was just what Mullins had wished for, Florida Pearl now found himself in the lead. In front fully half a mile from home, the danger was now all too obvious. Directly in the line of fire, he was there to be shot at by several of the leading fancies behind.

Watching through his binoculars from the stands, Willie Mullin's heart began to pound. This was what he was looking for and under gritted teeth, he whispered an order for Dunwoody to push him and bring his stamina into play. As the battle commenced out on the track, the jockey pushed and pushed from fully four furlongs out. So far, nothing had come to his quarters but there was a long way to go. He kept pushing and pushing.

They entered the home straight and Dunwoody could see the famous Cheltenham hill up in the distance. It was still a good distance out. Still nothing came to challenge and the horse and jockey were now in free flow. They were showing no sign of stopping and then the huge Irish roar went up from the packed stands. The adrenalin rushed through Richard Dunwoody's veins. Still nothing had come from the pack. He kept pushing with all his might knowing that the hill had found out so many in the past.

Florida Pearl was running at such speed that his jockey now knew it would take a great horse to beat them. As they approached the winning post, no sounds of flailing whips or ground breaking hooves could be heard.

Passing the winning line, all that could be heard was the deafening roar from the crowd. They had done it. The feeling was so sweet. The plan had been executed to perfection. The rest were run into the ground and it was five lengths back to the second horse (Arctic Camper ridden by Richard Johnson).

The dreams of Archie O'Leary and his wife Violet had been realised. A Cheltenham winner at last and money very well spent. As he dismounted, Richard Dunwoody said that the horse had a great future ahead and that he could be as good as another great bumper winner, Montelado.

Willie Mullins said that the horse was as good as his previous winner, Wither or Which. He also stated that Florida Pearl was now likely to go racing over fences rather than hurdles.

Following the great bumper win of Florida Pearl, the word 'special' was used a lot and it is easy to explain why. Great horses like Istabraq and Limestone Lad win successive races for a variety of reasons. The horse's breeding, his trainer and jockey spring to mind. Of course he must also have the ability but perhaps the most important reason is temperament.

To walk into a horsebox and be driven from Clare to Cork to race in a field and to win in your first ever race is some feat. Then to walk into a horse lorry and be driven from Carlow to Dublin and wait around all day and then win in front of 18,000 in your second race is impressive. But to travel across the Irish Sea to Cheltenham, then wait until twenty to six to race against twenty four of the best horses around and win again in front of 43,000 - that is the cool head of a champion.

While many Irish punters toasted the successes of Istabraq and Florida Pearl well into the night, Willie Mullins sat down to dinner at a Cheltenham hotel with Archie and Violet O'Leary. Already, they were planning the horse's next race. His bumper days were now over and he was now a big player entering into the big league.

It is a natural progression for bumper horses to graduate to hurdling. Most hurdlers then step up to chasing. In Florida Pearl's case, his next move was somewhat unorthodox though not unique or unusual.

After Istabraq won at Cheltenham, the word on the grapevine was that he was going for the Champion Hurdle the following year. He would therefore be targeting all the top hurdle races in Ireland. So taking on the speedy son of Sadler's Wells was not a viable option.

In truth, Willie Mullins never really favoured hurdles anyway. The sheer size, scope and stamina of Florida Pearl meant that he was a real natural chaser. Allied to the fact that he had beaten speedsters over two miles, he would be a big force over fences. Of course, that was providing he took to jumping fences well - and at speed.

Willie suggested to the owners that the horse should bypass the big Punchestown Festival and that he be put away for the rest of the season. After his summer rest, he would be schooled over fences in the late summer and early autumn. All going well, his first race over fences would again be at the Leopardstown Christmas meeting.

Schooling over fences in Carlow is one thing, it is quite another to jump fences in a race at speed. To make the grade as a top chaser, Florida Pearl would need to be able to do this.

When he lined up for the Farming Independent Beginners Chase on Monday 29th December 1997, the jury was out on whether such a big muscular horse could pass this latest test.

In contrast to his bumper win over fast ground on a mild spring day, conditions on the day of his chasing debut were a cause for concern. On a gloomy Christmas afternoon at Leopardstown, persistent rain made the ground heavy.

Initial doubts as to his ability to jump fences at speed were now compounded by the state of the track. It also made jumping that little bit more hazardous.

Richard Dunwoody did the sensible thing and immediately sent Florida Pearl into the lead in order to avoid trouble. As soon as he jumped the first fence, many questions were answered there and then. He pinged it and followed that by also jumping the next few brilliantly. There was never really a moment to worry about and the evens favourite came home twenty lengths clear of Tom Taaffe's Delphi Lodge.

Four wins from four starts and it was a spectacular performance to say the least. He did fiddle a couple of fences and he over jumped the last somewhat, but it was an impressive chasing debut.

After the race, a delighted Willie Mullins and Archie O'Leary announced that the horse would return to the same track the following month. He would have one more race over fences before returning to Cheltenham again.

One of the most impressed observers that day was Mike Dillon, representative for bookmaking giants, Ladbrokes. He offered odds of 25/1 about the horse winning the 1999 Cheltenham Gold Cup! Dillon was also quoted as saying:

"Every so often you see a horse that takes the eye and he is one. It was as impressive a debut as I've seen in years. He is clearly high class".

Another horse was boosting his growing reputation that day. The 1/6 favourite Istabraq won the Festival Hurdle so easily, Charlie Swan was seen looking around at least five times as they strolled up to the line. Those in the Florida Pearl camp had made the correct decision and there was no such looking back.

On Sunday 8th February 1998, Florida Pearl returned to the Foxrock venue. Barring a disaster, the Dr. PJ Moriarty Novices Chase was his prep race for Cheltenham.

Depending on his performance, a choice of three engagements awaited him in the Cotswolds. He would run in either the Arkle Chase, the Sun Alliance Novices or the Cathcart.

In a small field of five on 'tacky' ground, Florida Pearl again jumped impeccably. Two fences from home he was travelling easily. It just seemed a matter of Dunwoody pushing the button and the race was won.

He cruised into the lead at the last, but on landing he could not get Florida Pearl to stretch out. Boss Doyle, under a typical strong drive from Tony McCoy, got to within a length of him and all the way to the line the pair were involved in a right slog. Florida Pearl just held on to remain unbeaten.

There was a mixed reaction to the performance. Florida Pearl received seven pounds in weight from the second and so at level weights, the theory is that he would have been beaten. Many others were impressed at the way he battled it out and held off his more experienced rival.

Willie Mullins put forward a number of reasons for the narrow win. Before the race he was concerned that Florida Pearls blood tests showed that he was not a hundred per cent and he considered not running him. The ground was also sticky and he also said that the horse was a hundred pounds heavier than his Cheltenham bumper win.

Whatever the merits of his latest narrow win, Mullins announced that all going well, he would have the horse spot on for the Sun Alliance Novices Chase at Cheltenham just over a month later.

For Archie O'Leary, the horse had also repaid every penny he had paid for him. The £32,000 win brought his earnings from five wins to just under £60,000. In such a short time, Florida Pearl did not owe him a penny and it was now onwards to Cheltenham once more.

CHAPTER 3

PRIDE BEFORE THE FALL

When a good horse comes along, inevitably comparisons are made with the legendary Arkle. Such was the case with Florida Pearl. He was unbeaten, improving and had just recorded two very impressive wins over fences.

The potential was seemingly enormous. The Irish had been crying out for a real star chaser to emerge. Hopes were now high that at long last, a real champion had been found.

In previous years, Danoli and Doran's Pride had promised so much. Ultimately, they failed to deliver the goods. Both horses won many big prizes in Ireland but in England they came up woefully short. Then in 1996, Imperial Call won the Gold Cup to finally answer Ireland's calling.

It did not last. Although he was a real quality horse, he can probably be best described as a 'one hit wonder'. Trained by Ferdie Sutherland, both disappeared as quickly as they had arrived.

Nevertheless, appetites had been whetted. After the famine following Dawn Run's amazing success in 1986, the hunger for more Gold increased. Many in racing were literally salivating over Florida Pearl. Expectations grew and grew. The general excitement and anticipation were such that the media began to have a feast As a result, the general racing public began to look forward to what savoury goodies the big horse might bring to the table.

Florida Pearl fever forced bookmakers to quote odds of 25/1 about him winning the 1999 Gold Cup! But of more immediate concern was the Sun Alliance Novices Chase. When the bookies opened up their prices on that race, Florida Pearl was installed as 3/1favourite. Boss Doyle, the horse he beat at Leopardstown, was joint second favourite at 7/1 with the English horse, Escartefigue.

Just over a week before the race, Florida Pearl travelled to Leopardstown for his last serious piece of exercise before Cheltenham. He jumped over four obstacles alongside an experienced jumper and he out jumped him at every fence. Richard Dunwoody then worked him over a complete circuit of the course. When he asked him to quicken at the final bend, he accelerated very impressively.

Willie Mullins was thrilled with that piece of work. He told Archie and Violet O'Leary that they need worry no more about the horse's narrow win last time out. From what he and Dunwoody had observed, it was going to take a brilliant effort by an exceptional horse to beat their charge.

Word spread fast and as it did, punters latched on. Many made frantic phone calls to their bookmakers and the reaction from the layers was swift. The odds on Florida Pearl tumbled. The 3/1 had vanished and 7/4 was now the very best price available. On his way over to the big Festival, he was now carrying the tag of 'Irish Banker'.

Each year, as Cheltenham approaches, the Irish select their banker bet. As they travel in their thousands by air and sea, they all have in their minds an Irish horse that is a 'cert' to win.

Such a horse will carry their maximum bet. They will bet various sums of money on various horses. They will bet on other Irish horses and they will bet on English and perhaps even French horses. But Florida Pearl was the one they would pin all their hopes on - not to mention their hard earned money.

So, on Wednesday 18th March 1998, Florida Pearl was not alone the best bet of the day, he was the Irish Banker for the meeting. His was the name on everyone's lips. He was going to provide the expenses for the Irish at the three day extravaganza.

Thousands of punters were waving their wads in the faces of the worried bookmakers. So much money was wagered on him on that one day, that it surely surpassed the household budgets of an entire small Irish town.

Of course we all know that there is no such thing in racing as a certainty. You pay your money, you take your chance - and that's precisely what it is, a chance. In 1995, Harcon was seen as the banker. He also ran in the Sun Alliance but he was beaten by the outsider, Brief Gale.

However, many bankers do oblige and in the two years following Harcon's defeat, the Irish did celebrate. In 1996, they were spoilt for choice. Imperial Call was very popular at 9/2 when running away with the Gold Cup. He was just one of a magnificent seven winners for Ireland.

The banker was Whither or Which who was also trained by Willie Mullins. Accompanied by the famous Irish roars, he won at the generous odds of 3/1. Elegant Lord was also a popular winner in the Foxhunters.

A certain Istabraq was the banker in 1997 when he won the first race of the meeting. For the next three years he would also be the name on everyone's lips as he bagged an historic three Champion Hurdles.

In the first of that trilogy, run the day before Florida Pearls big test, he was something of an unknown quantity. When he stormed up the hill twelve lengths clear, he was only starting out on the road to immortality.

Now it was the turn of Florida Pearl. All eyes were glued to his every move. Betting slips were clutched tightly on the course, in bars and betting offices and in front of television sets in every corner of Britain and Ireland. As the long elasticised tape flicked back, and the starter shouted 'Come On', he was sent off the 11/8 favourite. On any other racecourse, he would have been at very prohibitive odds.

Early on, Dunwoody dropped Florida Pearl to the rear of the ten runner field. For the entire first circuit, they barely budged as they stalked those in front. The main reason for doing this was for to keep out of trouble. Novice chases are notorious for having fallers and various other mishaps. At the rear, horse and jockey could keep an eye on everything happening in front of them.

It proved to be a wise and correct decision. Two horses - Joliver and Ottawa - crashed out in the early stages. The aptly named, Fiddling the Facts, also put in a fairly hairy round of jumping and was very lucky not to have come down.

Coming to the business end of the race, Dunwoody and Florida Pearl made their move. But as they did so, Adrian Maguire and Escartefigue followed. They looked to be going ominously well.

In the betting market, Escartifigue also proved popular among English punters. If the Irish harboured great hopes for Florida Pearl, then the English were quietly confident about their horse upsetting the odds. When both entered battle two fences from the finish, echoes of Arkle v Mill House, Ireland v England were rekindled.

Florida Pearl was in front but he was strongly pressed on the outside by the English horse. The race was between the two with all other challengers burnt off. Legs and arms were in overdrive as both combinations of horse and jockey rose above cruising speed. The race was on. The fastest and strongest would win. A mistake would end the contest.

Down to the last fence and you could feel the millions of heartbeats create an electric current in the stratosphere surrounding two countries. Gritted teeth, eyes dilated, fists clenching dear dockets, fingers to mouths, hands on heads, screaming, shouting - the tension and excitement was all there.

On the inside, the white faced Irish favourite. On the outside, the white faced English second favourite. Their physiques were so similar they looked like brothers. Brothers in arms and approaching the last, legs and muscles were primed and ready. Both rose majestically and the tumultuous roar seemed to increase the spring in their jump.

Every man, woman and child seemed to be riding the race with Dunwoody and Maguire. As Florida Pearl was about to touch down, Escartefigue was halfway across the fence. The great Irish hope had a length advantage and just two other possible obstacles remained. A new distance of one furlong more and the fearsome hill which he had ascended before.

Flat out to the finishing line, both horses gave their all. At the winning post, it was Florida Pearl who had kept his advantage. He had also kept his unbeaten record - and his glowing reputation. A brave and battling challenger had been kept at bay by a distance of one and a half lengths.

The banker had prevailed to keep the wolves from the door. As a result, amid the scenes of joy, there were gasps of huge relief. In such great moments, money seems to be a ravaging, evil invader. But like gatecrashers at a party, it is a major player in helping to create the tension and fun. As Florida Pearl was led into the winners enclosure, the celebrations began.

A normally quiet and placid Richard Dunwoody grinned broadly as he urged the gathering crowd to sing. To the waiting media, he also gave his thoughts on the race:

"Adrian was going to make sure I got the trip as if he didn't get the trip he was going to get beat. The only doubt beforehand was just not having gone the 2miles 5furlongs before but Willie was confident he would get the trip. It was a great performance. He travelled very well and his jumping was great, very clever. He listened to everything I said and whenever I asked him for a long one, I got it".

A clearly delighted, and somewhat relieved, Willie Mullins added:
"People were expressing doubts about his staying ability but I think today he put paid to that. He's answered all his questions ok. I was happy with the ground today but he'll take any ground. He'll be back next year for the big one".

The big one Willie referred to was of course the Cheltenham Gold Cup. Those who had taken the ante post prices of 25/1 and 33/1 were now beginning to get very excited. After his win in the Sun Alliance, his odds were slashed to 10/1. The horse he beat, Escartefigue, was 14/1. They were the top novices around. A measure of how good they were was in the fact that the third horse, the French trained Fulip, was 20 lengths behind in that Sun Alliance.

So strictly on the formbook, both horses would fight out the finish of the 1999 Gold Cup. However, in between times, so much can happen and so much can go wrong. Another serious racehorse could also emerge. A year is a long time in horseracing.

After a well earned rest and summer holiday, Florida Pearl returned to work. The aim was to have him ready and as fit as possible for the Ericcson Chase at Leopardstowns Christmas meeting. As the race neared, and other potential challengers were scared off due to Florida Pearl's presence, it became clear that the race would be an intriguing one. Doran's Pride stood his ground and would run.

On the day after Florida Pearl's great Cheltenham win, Doran's Pride ran in the Gold Cup. He finished a very fast finishing third to Cool Dawn and was generally considered to have been very unlucky. He only finished just over a length behind the winner but he made a very bad mistake at the third last. Doran's Pride would therefore prove a real threat to Florida Pearl - not just in the Ericcson but to his glowing and growing reputation.

The race was building up into a potential thriller. Although only a small field, there were a couple of others capable of winning. Boss Doyle was a real tough stayer and from England came the grey, Suny Bay.

What made the race even more interesting was the fact that Tom Doran instructed Michael Hourigan to send Doran's Pride for the Ericcson. They also had an entry in the Hennessey two months later. So by taking on Florida Pearl, they were obviously confident and not swerving to avoid him.

Their plan suffered a slight setback however. Richard Dunwoody was Doran's Pride jockey after the tragedy that befell Shane Broderick. He was also the pilot of Florida Pearl so he had a dilemma and a big decision to make.

Whichever horse he chose to ride, in all likelihood he would never get the chance to ride the other again. On Monday, 14th December, exactly two weeks before the race, Dunwoody made his decision. He rang Michael Hourigan to apologise. His decision was to ride Florida Pearl.

If plans in Doran's camp were unsettled, then Mouse Morris the trainer of Boss Doyle was also left scratching his head. Tony McCoy, the regular rider, was required by his boss Martin Pipe at Chepstow the same day. In the end, Paul Carberry came in for the ride on Doran's Pride and Shay Barry was booked for Boss Doyle. Two very good young jockeys and the stage was now set.

In excess of 20,000 people turned up at Leopardstown to watch the big showdown. It was expected to be a two horse race but in racing, anything can happen. Such small fields can also cause confusion to jockeys if they cannot comprehend the tactics.

Boss Doyle was expected to set off and set a strong pace. If he did not do so, then Suny Bay was also a confirmed front runner. If both refused to make the running, then a 'muddling' race would ensue.

A muddling race, where no horse wants to make the running, would invariably present big problems to the top two in the race. Class horses generally like a truly run and fast race. If it became a muddle, and a slowly run affair, then most likely one of the top two would have to take up the running. If that happened, then the one making the running would be playing into the hands of the other. In other words, he would be there to be shot at.

In the event, they need not have worried. The small field set off at a good clip with the lead alternating between Boss Doyle and Suny Bay. The first casualty, and big surprise, saw Suny Bay run his race by halfway. He dropped tamely away and was well beaten when eventually coming to grief at the third last.

His jockey Graham Bradley later made a very memorable comment to journalists. He said his horse was, "beaten at halfway and was unconscious when he fell".

Boss Doyle was in front but was treading water when Doran's Pride eased up alongside and cruised past. Florida Pearl followed in behind and both opened up a huge gap on Boss Doyle. The crowd got their showdown. A broad buzz preceded a huge roar which rose up from the packed grandstands. The race was between the big guns.

At the final ditch, three fences from the finish, Dunwoody made his move. Sitting in behind, and just a couple of lengths back, he asked his horse for a big jump. Florida Pearl came crashing to the ground. Shock and horror on the faces of so many followed by awesome gasps and groans.

With the sudden injection of pace, perhaps Florida Pearl was caught in two minds at the fence. Paul Carberry, obviously hearing all the commotion, knew the race was over. He popped Doran's Pride over the last two for an easy win and a tremendous ovation from the crowd.

After the race came the post-mortems. Florida Pearl got up and seemed fine after the fall. Dunwoody was left bruising only a battered pride. He asked his horse to stand off and put in a big jump but he got a short stride in too close and the result was a nasty looking fall. Answering the 'what ifs' afterwards, the jockey said: "He travelled well and had jumped well. I was happy to track Paul but he took a chance and paid the price".

For the winner, plans had been fulfilled. It was straight back to Cheltenham for him and high hopes of atoning for his unlucky third in the previous attempt. For the faller, it was back to the drawing board. There were also uncertainties - not least his well being. Providing there were no ill affects, it was back to school for Florida Pearl. He would have to eliminate jumping errors if he was to be a serious Gold Cup contender.

A few days later, Willie Mullins gave his horse the all clear and a clean bill of health. Speaking to Irish Times reporter Michael Clower, he said:

"Florida Pearl was so well in himself when he got home that he ate up twice. I fed him not knowing that he had already had his supper. He cleaned up both feeds".

Depending on his schooling progress, Mullins nominated two races in early 1999 as possible targets. However, if both races were a little too soon, then he would run Florida Pearl in February's Hennessey.

Commenting on the fall at Leopardstown, he said: "I'm certainly not going to panic after one fall. It was just about the first mistake the horse has made in his life and had it been an ordinary fence, rather than a ditch, he might have got away with it".

Opinion may have been divided as to the outcome of the race if the fall had not happened. But there were now more questions than opinionated answers. The biggest question was the affect of that fall on the horse mentally. If he returned to races wary of fences and started to jump them slowly and carefully as a result, rather than at speed, it could mean the end of his racing career at the very top level. All eyes would be on Florida Pearl in his next race. The jury was well and truly out on this one.

CHAPTER 4

GOING FOR GOLD

There was no doubting that Florida Pearl's crashing fall at Leopardstown was a major setback. For the majority of observers, it was just fall and as long as there was no injury then it was just a matter of getting on with the next race. But to those closely associated with the horse, there were many concerns.

Two weeks after the Ericcson debacle, Willie Mullins schooled Florida Pearl. Initially, the signs were not good. Florida Pearl was not showing the same sparkle and exuberance that he had shown before. Somewhat understandably, he was very careful and deliberate at the schooling fences.

Gradually, and after a lot of hard work and persistence, horse and rider began to get the hang of things. By the end of the session, a relieved Mullins said:

"I took him up to my fathers place and Ruby Walsh rode him over the schooling fences. The horse jumped really well and he is back in great form". He then gave the horse the green light for the Hennessey at Leopardstown in February.

On a cold and overcast day, Florida Pearl faced another small field of just six rivals for the big race. The race was over a distance of 3miles for a prize fund of £100,000.

Some of the usual suspects lined up against him. Chief threat among them was Escartefigue. After the close race between them in the Sun Alliance, if Florida Pearl was not back to his best then this one would surely capitalise.

After a week of rain, the going was officially described as 'soft'. This was not seen as a major problem. Although he had won most of his races on good or faster going, he had beaten Boss Doyle in really soft ground. There were no excuses. As he had beaten most of the field before, Florida Pearl was a hot favourite at 8/15 with Escartefigue behind him in the market at 10/3.

The Ted Walsh trained Papillon, together with Bob Treacy, carried the field along at a good gallop. As expected, Dunwoody and Richard Johnson on Escartefigue sat in behind. The first casualty was Boss Doyle. He was pulled up and it later transpired that he pulled a shoulder muscle when dragging his hind legs through the second fence.

Going to the third last, Dunwoody made his move and joined the leaders. No mistake this time and going down to the second last he moved into the lead. He jumped it well and there was just the final fence to negotiate. All was going to plan. But just like the Sun Alliance, Escartefigue was sitting pretty in behind. It was the Cheltenham race all over again.

Jumping the last, Florida Pearl again rose just in front of the English challenger. Dunwoody was soon handed the advantage as it became apparent that Richard Johnson, not happy with his horse's response, began to brandish the whip. Like Cheltenham, the English combination threw everything at Florida Pearl but they could not peg him back. The winning distance of 2lengths was also an improvement on the previous effort.

While nominating the Gold Cup as the next target, Willie Mullins, while obviously delighted and very relieved, issued a few words of caution:
"Escartefigue ran a great race and the extra two furlongs at Cheltenham would worry me".
This view was echoed by David 'The Duke' Nicholson, trainer of the English horse:

"He has run a very good race today and the extra distance at Cheltenham just may suit him more than the winner. They are two very good horses and there is very little between them".

There were contrasting fortunes for the winning and second placed jockeys. A beaming Dunwoody said, "he was very good today and it's going to take a very good one to beat him at Cheltenham". A rather red faced Richard Johnson received a 3day ban from the stewards. He was deemed to have used his whip with, "excessive force and frequency".

On a lighter note, five other winning favourites that afternoon, had the bookmakers running for cover. Knife Edge 4/6, Alexander Banquet 1 /2, Nick Dundee 4/6, Limestone Lad 11/4 and Elegant Lord at 1/1 all advertised their Cheltenham claims. However, on course bookies Ladbrokes, amid much laughter, announced that they had run out of money to pay winning punters!

For the punters, many of whom laughed at this, there was also a sting in the tail awaiting them. There were 3,936 winning units of the £40,000 Jackpot and each received the paltry dividend of just £7.80. No doubt there were many players of the Jackpot who invested hundreds of punts in the hope of winning a very large sum. When the dividend was announced, many must have felt like not bothering to collect it!

Ladbrokes installed Florida Pearl as the 5/2 favourite for the Gold Cup after his impressive Hennessey win. Teeton Mill was next in the betting at 5/1 followed by Escartefigue 7/1, Cyfor Malta 8/1 and Dorans Pride at 10/1.

The odds on Dorans Pride were very attractive considering his win over the fallen Florida Pearl in the Ericcson. With over a month to the big race, it was building up into a fascinating Gold Cup.

Victory in the Hennessey stamped Florida Pearl's passport to Cheltenham for the third year running. This time he was to contest the greatest race in the National Hunt calendar.

The Gold Cup is the Premiership of the horseracing. Unlike the Grand National, which is a big Handicap, the Gold Cup brings together the classiest horses around. It was also a dream come true for Archie O'Leary. When he bought the horse from the Costello's, this was what he had paid good money for.

On Thursday, 18th March 1999, twelve horses lined up for the Gold Cup and a total prize fund of £250,000 sterling. The winner would pocket £150,000 with money going down to the sixth placed horse worth £3,000. Imperial Call, the 1996 winner, was pulled out due to a throat infection. Earlier, 1998 winner Cool Dawn was pulled out because of the ground conditions.

Florida Pearl was favourite and a measure of how popular he was can be gauged by the horses behind him in the betting. The Venetia Williams trained Teeton Mill had won his last five races. He won the English Hennessey by a massive 15 lengths and he also won the King George at Kempton where he beat Escartefigue.

After beating Florida Pearl last time, Dorans Pride had been rested for this race. Escartefigue was a hardened warrior with a big heart and was ready to do battle again.

Double Thriller represented up and coming trainer Paul Nicholls. He had won over the course and distance the previous year and he was also coming here as a winner of his last two races.

The Racing Post form verdict picked Dorans Pride. Their selection was due to the freshness of the horse as well as his fast finish the previous year. It also went on to say:

"A tremendous contest. Classy chasers Florida Pearl and Teeton Mill are the fastest in the field but if either has a weakness then it is probably in the stamina department. Florida Pearl may be the stronger stayer of the pair".

Heavy rain at the Gloucester track in the preceding days changed the going to 'good to soft'. As the starter called them in, the huge and expected roar went up from the crowd. Twelve jockeys manoeuvred twelve horses into a straight line in front of a long white tape. Close on fifty thousand people made a bee line for the nearest vantage point to watch the race.

Just before the start, bookies sensed that in such a competitive event, Florida Pearl was there for the taking. Several shouted odds of " 11/4 The Pearl ". Shrewd punters, unable to make up their minds, and looking for value, were suddenly tempted. One punter rushed in with a bet of £100,000 to win £275,000! Another followed suit with a wager of £50,000. Escartefigue also attracted some money. The highest recorded bet on him was £50,000 at 8/1 but before the race even began that punter was to be disappointed - the horse drifted to 11/1!

The course at Cheltenham is notorious. It is one of the toughest anywhere and that is why it takes a really special horse to win there. On an undulating track, the horses race flat out and in the process they negotiate the famous ditch, the downhill fence and the fence at the top of the hill. The mere mention of these fences by the commentator instils fear and worry into the viewer. Many a horse and jockey have been caught out by these fences. It is the sheer breakneck speed that usually forces the errors.

Having safely negotiated the fences, it is all uphill to the finish - a gruelling and punishing finale after 3miles 2furlongs. The mere mention of the hill by the commentator and, for the horse in front, the viewer fears the worst. Many have been caught in the shadow of the winning post. It is the fatigue and utter exhaustion that can be the final execution.

Shortly after 3pm, the starter, happy with the formation in front of him, let them off. The tape shot back and as it did, the most almighty roar swept across the Cotswolds. Ahead of them lay seventeen of the toughest fences in Britain and Ireland and a real test of a horse's stamina.

Senor El Betrutti, a grey trained by Susan Nock, made the running. The lead changed several times in the early stages. Double Thriller and Dorans Pride also took up the lead. Gasps of dismay greeted the first horse to bite the dust.

Second favourite Teeton Mill made a real mess of the seventh fence. Norman Williamson pulled him up at the ninth. He was immediately put into the horse ambulance. Later, the diagnosis of a bad tendon injury meant the beginning of the end for his racing career.

Back up front, Double Thriller and Dorans Pride were still disputing the lead. Although the Irish horse was in a prominent position as planned, his jumping was not at all good.

Paul Carberry had to sit and suffer as his mount jumped the fences very low. This resulted in him going through the top of some of them. This also meant that he was using up valuable energy and soon the combination were a spent force.

Going to the top of the hill, and its fearsome fence, Double Thriller went 2lengths clear as Dorans Pride back peddled. Safely through, and descending the hill, 66/1 shot Go Ballistic went in pursuit of the leader.

As they approached the third last, the race rested between just four runners. Escartefigue and some of the others market leaders were big disappointments and never struck a blow.

If David Nicholson was disappointed with his horse, then his heart must have been pounding seeing his other runner, Go Ballistic, ease past the tiring Double Thriller. By the same token, as Paul Nicholls saw his horse fading, he must have been so full of hope to see another of his runners enter the fray. See More Business, under a very patient ride from Mick Fitzgerald, was making good ground in behind.

At the third last, Go Ballistic rose in front and he was running the race of his life. Only two other horses could capture the Gold. See More Business went in pursuit and the Irish contingent could no longer contain themselves as Florida Pearl followed in third.

He opened up a big gap on the beaten Double Thriller in fourth. The huge crescendo of noise signalled the arrival of Dunwoody on the Pearl. With 66/1 and 16/1 shots in front of him, surely the race was his for the taking.

Alas, it was to prove a short lived effort. He flattered to deceive and moments later, thousands of voices were silenced as the distress signals went out from Dunwoody. They had no more to give. The tanks were emptying fast and punters now knew their fate. A great wail of wild emotion one moment, a great wave of whimpers and murmurs the next. The race was going to an outsider.

Memories of 100/1 shock winner Norton's Coin in 1990 were rekindled as Go Ballistic was 3lengths clear. Fitzgerald tried desperately to reel him in but the rank outsider was showing no signs of stopping in the hands of Tony Dobbin. As both horses came to the last, Go Ballistic jumped it in front. Florida Pearl was about 7 lengths back in third but was a beaten horse.

Responding to the strong urgings of his rider, See More Business ranged upsides the brave outsider. The pair fought out a tremendous battle all the way up the hill. No quarter was given with both jockeys flailing whips, arms and legs in a bid to win the greatest prize which they had never won before.

Gallant Go Ballistic ran his heart out. In the end it was not enough. It was See More Business who had a length in hand at the line. It was one of the tightest and best finishes to a Gold Cup.

Mick Fitzgerald who had been second in the race on Rough Quest, could so easily have been on the second horse. In the past, he had partnered Go Ballistic to six victories!

Sadly, it was not to be for Florida Pearl. He momentarily looked a big danger but finished 17lengths back in third. Double Thriller was a further distance back in fourth to complete a memorable day for Paul Nicholls.

The trainer also inflicted some heartache on a small bookmaker not far from his stables. As owner of the only bookmaking shop in the town of Shepton Mallet, John Chappell paid out nearly £14,000 in winning bets. He even paid one lucky punter £1,650 as a result of a £2.50 reverse forecast on the 16/1 winner and 66/1 runner up!

For connections of Florida Pearl, the £27,000sterling was at least some consolation. While the general view expressed by the media was that he did not stay the extra 2 furlongs, those closely connected with Florida Pearl were not happy with his well-being. After the race Richard Dunwoody revealed, "he looks quite stiff and was not moving right when I pulled him up (after crossing the line)". Willie Mullins concurred, adding:

"I was not happy with his jumping which was not as supple as I expected. As a result, he used the tank to get there and hadn't enough to get up the hill".

Using the word 'supple' was the first indication suggesting that Mullins feared that all was not right with his horse. He could not be sure but he definitely suspected that something was amiss. Two heads are better than one and together with Dunwoody's use of the word 'stiff', it was clear that in their eyes something was wrong with Florida Pearl.

Willie Mullins also suggested to reporters that as his horses were not firing, perhaps they were not spot on. By this he meant that there could have been an undetected sickness or virus in his yard. Florida Pearl soon recovered from his exertions and his next race would surely tell if there was a more serious underlying problem.

The Grand National Festival at Aintree had a suitable race in the shape of the Martell Chase. But it came too soon after Cheltenham. By chance, a brand new race had been entered into the Irish racing calendar. The Heineken Gold Cup, run over 3miles 1furlong at the Punchestown Festival, was a better alternative.

Other trainers saw that race as a possible answer to their problems as well. Dorans Pride and Escartefigue, both of whom ran abysmally at Cheltenham, were also entered. When the entries were complete, all three were still in the race. With Imperial Call in the field as well, it was an intriguing end of season race to say the least.

In hindsight, Mullins may have made a mistake. Florida Pearl never fired in the inaugural running of the Heineken. He finished a never threatening second to Imperial Call. The newspapers described his performance very aptly as 'lifeless'. Others had a point in suggesting that the horse was 'over the top' or 'off the boil'.

While his jumping was pretty good, he ran no race at all. Perhaps Willie Mullins should have put him away for the following season after his Gold Cup run. Perhaps the lure of Heineken's good prize money, as well as wanting to get to the bottom of his 'stiffness', were too tempting to resist.

The only good thing to come out of the Punchestown race was the fact that at least he confirmed the form with two of his big rivals. Dorans Pride again failed to sparkle and finished a long way adrift in fourth. The ubiquitous Escartefigue finished third. Also, the winner Imperial Call was pulled out of the Gold Cup, so he went into the Heineken as a very fresh horse. Perhaps things were not as bad as they first seemed.

A long summer holiday now awaited Florida Pearl. Connections could only wish that the break would have a positive affect. Any problems like viruses or muscle ailments would hopefully be eradicated in the lazy hazy months ahead. Florida Pearl, it was hoped, would return the following season firing on all of his powerful cylinders.

CHAPTER 5

HASSLED IN A HANDICAP

Florida Pearl went back into serious training in October. There were several options for his first race of the new season. The usual Leopardstown fixture was high on the list of priorities. Then another new race was added to the National Hunt fixtures. The James Nicholson Wine Merchant Champion Chase held all the right credentials and it was a possibility.

This new race at Down Royal was Northern Ireland's richest NH race. It was worth £60,000sterling which at that time amounted to £100,000punts. That in itself was a huge attraction but so too was the distance of 3m 1f.

Whichever race he went for would ultimately be decided by how he was performing at home in training. If he was showing the right signs, they would go for the race up north. If not, they would wait until Christmas.

Following a workout at the Curragh on Friday, 25th October, when many newspapers reported that he had disappointed, it was announced that Florida Pearl would head for Down Royal.

When the entries for the big race on November 6th were complete, the line up was impressive. Doran's Pride would once again take up the challenge as would the English horse, Strong Promise. He had been placed in the Gold Cup behind Looks Like Trouble.

Altogether seven horses went to post. Florida Pearl and Dorans Pride carried 11st 10lbs. They would both have to give 7lbs to Strong Promise and to Jessica Harrington's impressive young horse, Ferbet Junior. Francis Crowley's Moscow Express, winner of four races from his previous six, was set to receive 10lbs from the top two.

Some gloss was knocked off the race when Strong Promise was a late withdrawal because of the soft ground. The race was now billed as a match between the big two.

However, there were two notable changes. Richard Dunwoody was unavailable through injury and so Paul Carberry was given the ride. Michael Hourigan also announced that his son Paul was the new pilot for Dorans Pride.

Ferbet Junior set off out in front at a good pace. He took up a commanding lead and for such soft ground, it was a good gallop throughout. For most of the race Dorans Pride raced in second with Carberry tracking him on Florida Pearl. The only casualty early on was Moscow Express who fell at the eight.

Approaching the straight for the final time, Carberry made his move. He sent Florida Pearl up to join both Dorans Pride and Ferbet Junior. Then came a moment of drama and anxiety. Florida Pearl slipped on the flat but it was just a momentary blip and he soon regained his balance and composure.

Landing over the third last, he touched down in front of Dorans Pride. Long time leader Ferbet Junior quickly faded after his exertions. The expected showdown between the top two never materialised as Dorans Pride had no answers to Florida Pearl's sudden burst.

He stretched right away and popped over the final two fences for an easy win. The distance of 2lengths was very misleading as Carberry eased him right down well before the line.

Coming into the winners enclosure, they received a huge ovation from the crowd. Those present were probably expressing their relief that their star and great hope was back. Everywhere there were scenes of great joy and delight - not least on the face of Willie Mullins who then explained the rumours of a bad workout the previous week:

"All his homework, everything except the Curragh, was extremely encouraging. At the Curragh I just wanted Paul to see that he has a limited amount of fuel in the tank. He just got tired and I expected that".

For winning jockey Paul Carberry, just sitting in the saddle that day was an achievement in itself. Back in the Spring, he came close to losing his life. After a fall on the gallops, he tried to explain away the pain. But after collapsing, it transpired that he had internal bleeding. He was rushed to hospital and was only saved by emergency surgery!

That was not the end of matters. Doctors then advised him to rest through the summer. However, in a daredevil challenge, in the form of hand gliding from a bridge over the Liffey, he collided with a boat and broke his collarbone. Recalling that incident with Sunday Times reporter Jonathon Powell, he said with a cheeky grin: "it was supposed to be a flying canoe but it did not fly!".

Reflecting on the horse's performance in the race, Carberry told Ray Glennon of the Irish Independent: "I gave him a breather at the fifth last and then he went on again and jumped the third last in front. It was plain sailing after that apart from that slip on the flat. He jumped well and he also showed that he stayed the distance. We're back in with a shout for the Gold Cup".

Before a possible second crack at that race, Mullins nominated the John Durkan at Punchestown or Leopardstown's Ericcson or Hennessey as the next target.

The day got even better for Mullins - and for Archie O'Leary. Carrying the same colours as Florida Pearl, they ran a newcomer in the last race the Bumper. The horse's name was Tuesday and on that Saturday, he was an impressive winner in the hands of James Nash.

Of all the pessimism and doubt written about Florida Pearl, full marks must be given to Irish Times racing journalist, Brian O'Connor. In a piece which appeared on the morning of that Down Royal race, his words proved very prophetic and sensible:

"To call the seven year old a fallen hero says more about the expectations of fans than about the horse. Any horse that has achieved a rating of 165 and has been beaten only twice in completed races can hardly be classified as a failure.

"But Florida Pearl's potential had a nation in thrall last winter. The latest 'best since Arkle' was built up to be the second coming of Pegasus, and when he ultimately finished third in the Gold Cup Holy Grail, the disappointment was palpable. In short, we lost the run of ourselves. The most popular of the subsequent excuses was that he did not stay. This, about a Hennessey winner, is debatable.

"The majority of Willie Mullins horses didn't fire at Cheltenham, and its likely the real 100 per cent Florida Pearl didn't show up on Gold Cup day. If he shows up today, he will be very hard to beat".

It was decided to bypass the John Durkan in favour of the Ericcson at Christmas. Those in racing were to be very disappointed with the entries for the Leopardstown event. It was one of the poorest turnouts the race has ever seen.

Nevertheless, the race was to provide many talking points. If Paul Carberry was the hero of the hour last time, on this occasion he was to come in for some very heavy criticism.

In the small farcical field, the only horse of any real quality was the Ted Walsh trained Rince Ri. The race was really there on a plate For Florida Pearl especially after his impressive win at Down Royal. That fact was very much reflected in the betting ring. He was sent off at 4/7favourite with Rince Ri at 9/2.

In what was one of his finest exhibitions of jumping, Florida Pearl met every single fence spot on. Watching the race, connections could not have been any happier with the way things were going. But to their horror, he lost the race! As Paul Carberry passed the post in second, he must have wished the ground would swallow him up.

Many observers felt that it was jockey error that led to the neck defeat by Rince Ri. Jumping a superb round, Carberry sat motionless as they negotiated the last few obstacles. In racing terms, they were 'cruising' and it seemed like only a matter of time when the button was pressed to speed past the other horse.

Rince Ri was hard at work especially after an horrendous mistake and he was lucky to stay on his feet. Popping over the last, Carberry was content to bowl along beside Rince Ri. He was being cheeky and he fully expected his horse to lengthen when he asked him.

It was so reminiscent of Pat Eddery aboard El Gran Senor in the 1984 Epsom Derby. On that occasion, Eddery cruised up alongside Christy Roche on Secreto fully two furlongs out. Looking around and around, he was toying with the opposition. But when he pressed the button, there was nothing left. Panic then set in and in a driving finish, the pair lost by a short head!

The same thing happened here. On the flat after the last, Carberry lobbed along beside the other horse. Halfway up the straight, he then asked Florida Pearl to lengthen but there was no response. He was very leaden-footed in the gluey ground.

Both horses were tired and were running up and down in the same spot. They seemed to be running in slow motion. Urgency required, Carberry pushed and pushed but however much he tried, he failed.

Looking rather sheepish afterwards, Carberry came in for a lot of stick. Punters vented their anger and that was not the end of the matter. Seeing what had happened, Channel 4's John McCririck was very vociferous in condemning the jockey's antics. The jockey later defended himself insisting that the horse found nothing. He also added that the horse was not fully fit and the ground was very sticky.

Mistakes do happen and after all, there is nothing certain in this game. In truth though, it would be hard to see McCoy or Johnson cruising alongside another horse at the business end of a race. Similar to the Pat Eddery case, many felt that, Carberry should have sent his mount into the lead much sooner. The dreadful haymaker from Rince Ri should also have been a signal to set sail for home. Instead, every opportunity was afforded to the winner to get back in the race.

Willie Mullins, perfect gentleman as he is, refused to blame his jockey. If anything, he concurred with Carberry's reference to Florida Pearl's fitness. Mullins was taking the blame himself by saying that he 'had left a bit to work on with the horse'. In other words, he did not have him fully primed or fit. It was now back to the drawing board and a race against time to get the horse ready for a second crack at the Gold Cup.

A huge surprise was in store when Florida Pearl's next engagement was announced. It was widely anticipated that the next target would be the Hennessey in February. Instead, it was decided to run him in a Handicap Chase! His target was the BAX Handicap at Leopardstown on January 23rd, 2000.

Many felt that by taking this easy option it was a means to giving the horse back some much needed lost confidence more so than getting another race into him. There was never a dull moment in the Florida Pearl soap opera which was being cast almost every week in the press. The BAX race, a stroll in the park as far as most people were concerned, was to provide another episode full of surprise.

Lumbered with top weight, Florida Pearl was conceding weight to all in the field. In Grade 1 races he ran in, he was used to carrying 12st. In this race, he would be conceding two and three stone in weight to some of the others.

So a horse running off 10st would be nearly 30lbs lighter than Florida Pearl. In terms of quality, such a horse could not live with him. But weight can make the difference and very often it does.

Nobody really expected him to lose but they were in for quite a race. A few jumping errors did not help his cause and coming to the last fence he was seen to be struggling. Over the last, and on the level, it looked like a lightweight on the outside had his measure and was about to swoop past. Great credit to Florida Pearl though as he battled like a lion and got up to win by a short head.

The horse that was on the outside was none other than Amberleigh House. He went on to win the world's greatest race, the Grand National, in 2004. That day he was receiving a massive 40lbs from Florida Pearl. On the face of it, the performance looked poor and very unimpressive. Seeing what Amberleigh House went on to achieve, it now makes very good reading.

The thrilling finish was fought out between two brothers - Philip and his older brother Paul Carberry who was redeeming himself after the Ericcson debacle. Willie Mullins gave this reaction after the race:

"At least he picked up and battled back because I thought he was going to be passed. Paul said he made a mistake down the back and lost his confidence a bit but when he got a kick in the ribs at the third last, he jumped much better".

Bookmakers were far from impressed. Almost all of them in unison pushed him out in the Gold Cup betting. It was then announced that he would contest the Hennessey. Any change in that plan and he would go over to England for Ascot's Shogun Chase. Before leaving the racecourse, Mullins also added:

"At least he's back to a bit of form and I hope we have no setbacks from now on".

As Hennessey day arrived on February 6th, Dorans Pride was there again along with his Ericcson conqueror, Rince Ri. There was to be no soft option this time. It was a small classy field and the result of this would tell so much.

There were also two other interesting runners. Former 'People's Champion' Danoli was returning after a long layoff. His Song was running after having had a soft palate operation.

Bob Treacy went off in the lead with Buck Rogers also having his moments. Somewhat surprisingly, Florida Pearl joined the leader before halfway. Fully eight fences from home, he was up there taking a hand at the head of the field. It was also very evident that he was looking fit and strong and was full of exuberance. He was also jumping superbly.

Five fences from the finish, he stormed into the lead. Dorans Pride went in pursuit and coming to the third last it was again between the two. All others were well and truly stuffed. Danoli was a well beaten horse when unshipping Tom Treacy at the third last. Rince Ri however was making ground stylishly from the back of the field. But as the big two injected more pace, his effort also petered out.

Hard as Dorans Pride tried, he was fighting a losing battle. Florida Pearl powered away under a much more industrious and workmanlike Carberry. They met the last perfectly and powered away to the line to record a 6length win. Rince Ri was a distant third. It was one of his most impressive performances in that, it wasn't so much the field he beat, but his aptitude and determination in doing so.

How the mood had changed from the previous weeks and months. The atmosphere was charged with positivity and satisfaction and everybody wanted to express this.

First there were the bookmakers. They slashed his price back down to 5/1second favourite for the Gold Cup. Next came the newspaper hacks. They surrounded connections in the winners enclosure looking for quotes. Previously they had written uncomplimentary pieces and now they were championing the horse once more.

Winning jockey Paul Carberry could not hide his delight. He could not wait to say, 'I told you so' and he just couldn't resist a swipe at one of his main detractors. With reference to the controversial defeat by Rince Ri he said: "This shows how unfit Florida Pearl was that day and Mr.McCririck might realise that now ".

Beaming owner Archie O'Leary also had a swipe when
he bellowed out:

"A few people are going to have to go back to writing
gardening columns".
No such swipes from the ever laid back Willie Mullins.
In a near faultless exhibition of jumping he simply said:
"Nobody could ever ask for more than that".

Putting a dampener on any suggestions that Carberry
had received a rap on the knuckles, he also added:
"The horse did all the talking and I told Paul to ride him
whatever way he wanted".

Tickets were now booked for Cheltenham. After that
display, he looked a really serious racehorse once more.
For probably the first time, connections were much
more relaxed and were genuinely looking forward to the
big day. Archie O'Leary explained:

"He was over hyped. He became like the sliced loaf, the
next Arkle and all that. Every second day there were
people looking for a comment and it got to the people.
Then when he was beaten, a lot of the correspondents
gutted us. I wasn't cross about it, just disappointed.
Now it's the turn of Gloria Victis and See More
Business to be hyped to hell".

Echoing what a lot of other observers had witnessed,
O'Leary also went on to say:

"He seems to be a leaner and tougher animal this time.
For the first time in eighteen months, I'm seeing him
attack his fences the way I know he can. They say he
wont get up the hill but he got up it in the Sun Alliance
and he's two years older now".

Down through the years, there were many barren years
when Ireland could not even muster a single horse good
enough to run in the Gold Cup. Now the days could not
pass quickly enough in the countdown to the 2000 Gold
Cup.

The whole of Ireland were anticipating great things
from Florida Pearl. But there were two other Irish
challengers. In a field of twelve, Rince Ri and Dorans
Pride meant that the Irish had a quarter of the line up.

As someone who made a very good living from selling
insurance, Archie O'Leary obviously had a very good
way with words. So it was quite fitting that as the big
day dawned, the proud owner had some final and fitting
words to say:

"It'll take some horse to beat him but it depends on the
horse pinging on the day.
On Gold Cup day some horse always pings. I just hope
it will be our ping!".

CHAPTER 6

THE YEAR OF TROUBLE

Prestbury Park, Gloucestershire - otherwise known as Cheltenham. In the heart of the hilly green Cotswolds, it's a real tourist attraction in mid March. Close to fifty thousand people descend upon its picturesque countryside for three successive days each year. Many carry binoculars but this is no bird watching sanctuary. It is a gambling mad paradise.

Of course betting is not just restricted to those present at the course. Hundreds of thousands of people like to bet on these races in betting offices in their towns and cities. Then in the late 1990's, telephone and credit card betting took off in a big way. Bookmakers saw a huge market potential here and so they decided to offer special free bets in order to attract new customers.

They started by offering new clients free bets worth £10 or £20 provided they opened a new account with them. Indeed things have now progressed so far that, at the time of writing this, a leading Irish bookmaker offered new accounts 100euros in free bets! On the Wednesday before the Gold Cup, one such customer was about to hit the jackpot.

A man named Jim Crowe, from Henley in London, rang Ladbrokes to open an account. He wanted to place bets at Cheltenham to the value of £20 for himself and his wife. He was actually totally unaware of a free special bet. Compliments of Ladbrokes, Jim was informed that he could have a £40 Straight Forecast on any race that day.

To win with such a bet, you must pick the first and second horse past the post in that order. It is actually very hard to do. To pick a winner is hard but to pick a winning forecast is even harder. Not doing things by half, Jim went for a forecast on the 26runner Coral Cup! It is probably one of the most difficult races in Britain to get the winner - never mind the forecast.

His selections, Whats Up Boys and Native Dara came up trumps. Jim was not just lucky on account of the win, he was also lucky as there was only a neck separating them. But their starting prices of 33/1 and 25/1 meant that he and his wife were about to get even luckier. The forecast paid £660.14p to a £1stake. From nothing, and multiplied by Ladbrokes £40, Jim picked up a cool cheque for £26,405.60p!

At Cheltenham, every man and woman present is a player in pursuit of a winning flutter. A win such as Jim's is what they all dream about. It is a game where you win or lose - there is really no such thing as a draw. Its as simple as black or white. On the board, in the front line, the horses are the pawns. You pay your money and you take your chance.

One of the biggest bets on Gold Cup day was placed on
the Stayers Hurdle just before the big race. Popular Irish
horse Limestone Lad was the subject of a monster bet.
A professional punter walked up to rails bookie Fred
Williams and placed £100,000 on him at 7/2. If the
horse won, he would win £350,000.

After a brave bid by the Irish horse, the punter lost.
Bacchanal spoiled the party but only by a diminishing
length. Limestone Lad's jockey Shane McGovern then
lodged a bizarre objection to the winner. It was bizarre
because there seemed little or no interference. The
stewards found likewise and fined McGovern £65 for
wasting their time!

Through the winter, and in the days before the big race,
See More Business was a warm 6/4favourite. Gloria
Victis was second favourite after he had won the Racing
Post Chase very impressively. On the day however,
both drifted in the market. See More Business went off
the 9/4favoutite while Gloria Victis was 13/2. The
money came for both Florida Pearl and Looks Like
Trouble who were backed into 9/2joint second
favourites.

It turned out to be an error strewn and tragic race. Of the
twelve that started, only six would finish. Gloria Victis
lead them all a merry dance for the first circuit.
However, his novicey ways and inexperience showed as
he tended to jump to his right. By doing this he was
losing ground at each fence.

Passing the stands and going out on the final lap, See More Business took it up. The crowd momentarily got excited and hoped the horse could retain his title. It was to be his only really showing. Gloria Victis regained the advantage. During the race, Ever Blessed as well as Go Ballistic and The Last Fling were pulled up. Tullymurry Toff unseated rider.

Downhill to the third last fence and it was here that all the real drama unfolded. Rince Ri unseated Ruby Walsh and he tried acrobatics to stay on but gravity dictated otherwise.

But one of the worst tragedy's ever witnessed took place at the next, the second last. The sketchy jumping of Gloria Victis was finally found out and he and Tony McCoy bit the dust. It quickly became apparent that something was dreadfully wrong.

A green screen was put around the horse to shield people from observing the terrible injuries that had been inflicted. The horse was then taken away in an ambulance for further assessment. However the state of the injuries to the cannon and sesamoid bones were such that they were beyond repair.

The owner and trainer explored every option as to whether the horse could be saved. Sadly he could not and he had to be put down. Everyone connected was devastated and it would take Tony McCoy along time to get over it.

Back in the race and Florida Pearl also made a mistake at the third last. He was not helped by the mayhem going on around him. But he then moved nicely into contention and after the fall of Gloria Victis, it looked like a two horse race for the Gold Cup.

Bedlam ensued as Looks Like Trouble was tackled by the great Irish hope and it was Florida Pearl who just touched down in front. It was the same noise levels as if a goal had been scored at Croke Park. All the new found confidence, everyone so relaxed beforehand - it finally looked like it was going to be their day.

Approaching the last and it was so close. Archie and Violet were hoping he would ping. Both horses leapt the last in great style accompanied by increased decibel levels. Richard Johnson and Looks Like Trouble had the slightest advantage on landing.

It was no more than half a length and with the hill to negotiate, that lead was nothing. The year before, Go Ballistic led by the same margin but lost out in a thriller. Was the same thing about to happen here. Florida Pearl also had the edge in experience.

On the climb for home, for a fleeting moment it looked like the white-faced giant would swoop past. Then it vanished. So too did Looks Like Trouble as Johnson got an electrifying response and they careered away for an impressive 5length win. So near again for Florida Pearl and he had to settle for silver after bronze the year before.

In the end, he had to fend off the fast finishing third placed horse Strong Promise by a neck. See More Business also put in his best work in the closing stages and was another length behind in 4th.

One horse who ran a blinder was 150/1 rank outsider, Lake Kariba. He was only another neck behind in 5th after at one stage looking like he would be a big threat.

A dramatic race full of talking points - not least the death of Gloria Victis. Many felt the six year old was too young and inexperienced to run in the race. The Racing Post also felt a little guilt after urging connections to 'GO FOR IT' in the days before the race.

It was also perhaps the first real start of a raging debate as to whether or not Florida Pearl got the Gold Cup trip. That was set to run and run with even jockeys and trainers split fifty- fifty on it.

Oddly, those in the Florida Pearl camp were feeling emotions of disappointment and delight at the same time. After the race Willie Mullins said there were no excuses: "I was delighted with him. He did what we went to do and that was to beat those who beat him last year and we did that. A new kid on the block, I'm afraid, came and beat us. He had every chance and we were just beaten by a better horse. We don't mind that. I think he got the trip all right".

Paul Carberry, who only passed himself fit to ride after physiotherapy on an injured back, was also very upbeat and gave another interesting view:

"I suppose we were a bit unlucky because we missed out one fence early on and then blundered badly three out which didn't help when it came to the home straight. I think he stayed the trip but it was the errors that took their toll".

Tracey Gilmour, Mullins head girl, reported Florida Pearl in great form next morning. If he continued in that vein then his next race would be the Martell Cup at Aintree and/or the Heineken at Punchestown.

Also next day, Tony McCoy rode the first winner at Folkestone. He was asked by the Racing Channel about the death of Gloria Victis to which he gave this reply: "To be honest, I don't really like talking about it…..it is probably the saddest thing that has happened to me in racing…..he was an exceptional horse and it hurts you more with horses like that".

Subsequently, Aintree and Punchestown were given a wide berth. Just as well for the Martell Cup claimed the life of Strong Promise who had been placed in two Gold Cups. That tragedy was one of four on one of Aintree's darkest days. It only served to add extra fuel to a fiery campaign by animal rights protesters who were very active back then.

In the end it was decided to put him away and out to grass for the summer. After silver and bronze, it was to be hoped that the following season would finally bring gold.

Down Royal's James Nicholson was the first confirmed target for the 2000/2001 season. In the second running of the event, Florida Pearl would be out to make it two from two.

The race was due to be run on November 11th but bad weather made the track unfit for racing. So the clerk of the course postponed the two day meeting for a week. It was actually just the beginning of a season that would bring other postponements and setbacks.

Plans and preparations for Florida Pearl were also suffering disruptions. Three days before that decision to defer racing for a week, Willie Mullins was experiencing problems of a similar nature as he stated: "The plan is still very much to go north. However, I would have liked to have given him a bit of schooling but that hasn't been possible because of the weather".

Exactly one week later, on a little known racecourse in Northern Ireland, a big Gold Cup rematch was on when Looks Like Trouble was confirmed a starter. Not surprisingly, it drew a huge crowd. Bookmakers could not separate the pair in the betting and they both went off as 5/4joint favorites.

The race turned out to be a mismatch. Florida Pearl looked good on the first circuit of the race but then he blew up and could only finish fourth of the five runners. Looks Like Trouble, who hadn't looked altogether at ease either, was left to go away for an easy win.

Fourth of five was the worst ever finish by Florida Pearl up to this point. With the original meeting abandoned, and with Mullins not happy with his preparation, it was clear that he was not fully in tune. In hindsight, it may have been better and wiser to have waited for the Leopardstown Christmas meeting.

The poor performance at Down Royal was nothing to do with new jockey Ruby Walsh. He was standing in for the injured Paul Carberry. But things were about to get worse. Three weeks after that debacle, the horse was confirmed as a runner in the John Durkan Memorial Chase at Punchestown. Only four runners went to post and it looked an easy assignment.

The ground, officially described as 'soft/heavy', was not ideal. But Florida Pearl had proved in the past that he had the stamina and the experience of such conditions to more than cope. The Arthur Moore trained Native Upmanship handled the ground even better and got up to win by a head! The shock, horror, pain and embarrassment had come home to haunt again.

After Rince Ri, Amberleigh House and the flop up north, this was another huge setback. Though connections were not to know it at the time, looking back now they can draw some degree of comfort from that race.

Just like the two horses mentioned, Native Upmanship would go on to reach the very top. He was placed in Cheltenham's Queen Mother Champion Chase as well as winning at the big Aintree meeting in 2002.

The head-scratching over Florida Pearl was now starting over again - just when it looked like his great run in the Gold Cup would be a platform for more success. Something was not right but Willie Mullins, hard as he tried, could not get to the bottom of it.

Perhaps it was time to break the monotony of his routine. Maybe a change in his race entries was needed. After a good heart to heart, Archie O'Leary and Willie Mullins agreed to give the horse a fresh challenge.

Florida Pearl would now be on his way to the South of England instead of the usual pattern of racing at Leopardstown during the Festivities. The King George VI Chase at Kempton Park is the biggest race staged during Christmas. It also attracts the very best horses.

First staged in 1937, great horses like Mandarin, Mill House, Arkle, Silver Buck, Wayward Lad, The Fellow, One Man and See More Business have won it. The great Desert Orchid won it a record four times.

For the Millennium King George, Florida Pearl was seeking to redeem his reputation. It was hoped that the unusual trip across the water, in the depths of winter, would stimulate him back to his best.

Nine runners went to post. Some of the usual suspects, like See More Business and Go Ballistic, were in opposition. Just as in the previous season's Gold Cup, those two also finished first and second in the previous King George.

One of the more unfamiliar aspects facing Florida Pearl was the course. Kempton is known as a very flat and fast track. It is probably ahead of Ascot as the fastest in Britain.

As a good fast galloper, it was thought that he would handle it and that it would probably even suit him. See More Business was the real course specialist however. He was bidding to win it for the third time after victories in 1997 and 1999.

As a warm up for the race, he absolutely trounced his three rivals in the Charlie Hall at Wetherby two months earlier. On the strength of that, and being a course and distance winner, he was the warm favourite at 6/4.

French raider, First Gold, was the 5/2 second favourite. His trainer Francois Doumen had a tremendous record in the race. He won the race on four previous occasions. In 1987 he became the first French trainer to win it when Nupsala triumphed. The Fellow gave him back to back wins in 1991 and 1992 and two years after that, he won it for the fourth time with Algan.

Florida Pearl was next in the market at 11/2 and then there was a big gap to Edredon Bleu at 12/1. Trained by Henrietta Knight, this fellow was a winner of the Queen Mother over 2miles at Cheltenham. A real speed merchant, there were real doubts as to whether he would have the stamina to last the fast 3 miles at Kempton.

Unlike the 12st they carry in the Gold Cup, most of the horses here carry 11st 10lbs. The exception was Lady Cricket. As a female she was entitled to carry an allowance of 5lb less. Trained by champion trainer Martin Pipe, and ridden by champion jockey Tony McCoy, it was also felt that she would struggle to get the trip.

The front running Edredon Bleu took up the lead early on. He was closely followed by Beau, See More Business and First Gold. The pace, as is generally the case in this Christmas spectacular, was furious. Already there were several horses struggling and it soon became apparent that the favourite See More Business was not doing so well.

He was giving Mick Fitzgerald some really anxious moments. His jumping was sloppy and he was ploughing through some of the fences. Florida Pearl was also finding it tough going. He made a bad mistake early on and as a result, he had a fair amount of ground to make up. Ruby Walsh eventually got him back on an even keel and with a circuit to go, they were still in the race.

Down the back straight with six fences to jump, Edredon Bleu was still out in front. Considering the question marks over his stamina, he was running a blinder. First Gold was travelling very well in behind under Thierry Doumen. Not going at all well was See More Business. After all his errors, he had nothing left to give.

As expected, a few fences later Edredon Bleu ran out of gas. But Florida Pearl was making good ground in behind along with the Venetia Williams trained Bellator ridden by Norman Williamson.

Approaching the second last, the race was about to be sealed. Thierry Doumen asked First Gold for a long one and the result was spectacular. A colossal jump brought gasps of amazement from the big Bank Holiday crowd and he galloped down to the last with clear daylight to the rest.

After safely popping over the last, the £87,000 first prize was in the bag. All that remained was the battle for the minor placings. Following a shaky start, Florida Pearl ran on past tiring and non-staying horses to get second. He finished 10lengths behind the winner with Bellator 11lengths behind him in third.

By any standards, it was not a great King George. It will probably be remembered for the brave and mammoth leap by the winner at the second last down the fast straight. But history had also been made. Francois Doumen had won the race for the fifth time. This equalled the record set by the great Fulke Walwyn between 1947 and 1971. Willie Mullins was magnanimous in defeat when he said:

"He kept on galloping and if the winner hadn't been there, he would have been an easy winner. There are no excuses. We just met a better horse on the day".

Although nothing was definite until seeing how Florida Pearl came out of the race, it seemed certain that the Hennessey back at Leopardstown would be his next race.

In that, he would also be aiming to equal a record as he was going for a third win in a row. He really had to get back to winning. The seconds were piling up. So also was the pressure - and it was mounting.

A young and gangly Florida Pearl wins in the Clare colours of the
Costello's, Lismore 96

Florida (R. Dunwoody) is different class in the Champion
Dumper, Cheltenham 1997

Packed stands watch Dunwoody guide The Pearl to beat Escartifigue in
the Sun Alliance Novices Chase
at Cheltenham in 1998.

Safely over and plodding through the mud for a hat-trick of
Hennesseys in 2001 with Alexander Banquet in front and Dorans
Pride/Commanche Court behind.

A huge leap from The Pearl in the James Nicholson at Down Royal

Heineken Gold Cup April 2002 and Florida jumps majestically in
contrast to the others.

Florida Pearl beats Escartefigue again to land the first of his Hennessys in 1999.

Paul Carberry and Florida cantering towards another Grade 1 in the John Durkan, Punchestown 2001

Touching down and ready for a real duel up the run-in for the
2001 King George

Florida (B. Geraghty) wins the Martell Cup at Aintree by
11 lengths in 2002

Enjoying Heineken success at Punchestown 2002 are B. Geraghty, Archie & Violet O'Leary, Tracey Gilmour and Willie Mullins

Another mighty leap (R. Johnson) on way to winning Norman's Grove, Fairyhouse 2004.

Cantering to the start for a record breaking win in the Hennessy,
Leopardstown 2004.

Richard Johnson urges Florida on for victory preceded by the loose
Harbour Pilot.

Harbour Pilot about to fall and Florida gallops on for record 4th win
in the Hennessy

4 is the magic number, as shown by a delighted Richard Johnson
and Tracey Gilmour.

CHAPTER 7

DUEL IN THE CROWN

Worrying news hit the entire horseracing industry in early 2001. An outbreak of Foot and Mouth disease in Britain spread right to the south of England. Although Ireland was as yet not affected, there were very real fears that British racing would be cancelled. If this happened, then Irish racing would also suffer.

In Ireland during the months of December, January and February, racing in Ireland is all geared towards Cheltenham. Many of the races are seen as trials for the big Festival and almost every owner, trainer and jockey wants to be there. Thousands of punters have booked tickets, travel and accommodation while bookmakers and the media also have big parts to play.

Race goers at Leopardstown's Hennessey meeting in February, all had an opinion on the matter. The majority felt certain that the disease would reach Ireland. The most common view seemed to be that if it did reach these shores, it would be carried on the wind from Wales! But for the time being, life went on as normal. In the Florida Pearl camp, a big job had to be done.

A field of seven went to post for the Hennessey with Alexander Banquet and Commanche Court other notable runners. Needless to say, regular sparring partner Dorans Pride was also in the race. Such was the quality that over 16,000 people braved the elements to watch the race. Mind you, the grey murky conditions made viewing a little difficult.

Nick Dundee took up the running at an early stage but disaster soon struck. At the fifth fence, Norman Williamson asked him for a big one but he just galloped right through the fence.

Gasps of horror bellowed out from the stands as the horse almost did a complete sommersault. Not for the first time with Nick Dundee, Williamson had to grab the horse and untangle the reins from around his girth to save him from any further injury.

The fall brought back painful memories of the horse's near fatal fall at Cheltenham in 1999. This was his third start since that dreadful day and thankfully, he did not pick up any further injury. It was another blessing for horse and jockey and on this occasion, the very soft ground almost certainly saved his life.

Just as Paul Carberry had done previously, Richard Johnson sent Florida Pearl to the front fully seven fences out. The rest of the field looked to be struggling in the ground and the race looked like his for the taking. But as the pair entered the straight, it became apparent that the conditions were beginning to take their toll and the horse's stride began to slow.

Over the last and on the run in, Johnson began to send out distress signals. He had to get very serious with Florida Pearl who was running up and down on the spot. In behind, Barry Geraghty on Alexander Banquet could see and sense the panic. He worked furiously to reel in the leader. The gap was closing fast.

From looking like the race was over after the penultimate fence, the crowd felt an upset was imminent. The neutrals cheered on the outsider while the vast majority were willing the favourite on through the boggy conditions. The post came not a moments too soon for Florida Pearl. He had a rapidly diminishing 2 lengths to spare over the gallant runner-up.

It was a major triumph for Willie Mullins. He had saddled the first two and it also meant that Florida Pearl now equalled the record of Jodami. The English horse, trained by Peter Beaumont, also won the race three times between 1993-95. In the race, Dorans Pride ran his usual honest race and finished a further 9lengths back in third. Commanche Court, in ground he detested, was a further 14lengths back in 4th. Third favourite Native Upmanship was always behind and was pulled up just before the last fence.

Incidentally, Richard Johnson replaced Ruby Walsh in that race as Ruby had been injured in a bad fall at Naas the previous week. Afterwards, the victorious trainer could not wait for another crack at the Gold Cup when he said:

"He put in a few sloppy jumps at Kempton but today his jumping was immaculate.
If he puts in that sort of performance at Cheltenham next month then I think he'll be in with a big shout of making it third time lucky".

The winning jockey, realising his good fortune in getting the ride, also threw his hat into the ring in a bold effort to keep it as he said:

"If he goes to the Gold Cup in that sort of form, everyone will have to fear him as well as First Gold. The way I see it, First Gold, See More Business and Florida Pearl are the big three. Depending on what Ruby rides, the Florida Pearl people have my number and my agents number".

A couple of weeks later, his cheekiness was rewarded when he received that cross- Channel call. In effect, owner Archie O'Leary made the decision. He instructed Mullins to 'jock off' Ruby Walsh and replace him with Johnson. This came about after Ruby could not give a firm commitment to ride the horse as he was also due to ride his father's Commanche Court in the Gold Cup.

The trainer explained the tough decision to Pat Keane of The Examiner:

"I thought Ruby would ride Florida Pearl. I am of the opinion, obviously, that Florida Pearl has the best credentials of the Irish horses but clearly, Ruby thinks differently. I'm a little surprised that he didn't give the commitment but it's his decision and we have an excellent replacement in Richard Johnson. This will not affect my relationship in any way with Ruby".

Although it was a bit of a struggle in the ground, bookmakers were still impressed enough to trim his odds for the Gold Cup. Generally he was now a 10/1 chance from 12.

Alexander Banquet was also making an impression on the layers. He was cut to 14/1 from 25. If the going turned out to be soft at Cheltenham, many shrewd observers felt that he would have a big chance. Before all that, there was still the big matter of Foot and Mouth.

On 26th February, Willie Mullins, as Chairman of the
Trainers Association in Ireland said:

"I'm very apprehensive about racing taking place. The
next 24hours will tell a lot but I'm very pessimistic.
When I heard that the disease had spread to Devon that
really worried me as it is now in the four corners of
England".

Next day came some bad news. A temporary ban on
racing was introduced from 27th February until further
notice. It actually resumed at Sandown just over a week
later but after the ban, racing really became optional.

Some racecourses closed, some raced. However many
trainers decided against running their horses. Although
the disease cannot affect horses, the majority cited their
support for the suffering farmers as the main reason for
their actions.

Very soon, the situation would deteriorate further when
it was confirmed that the disease had spread to a farm
close to Cheltenham. Despite this, officials at
Cheltenham kept announcing that the Festival would go
ahead. This was also stressed by Willie Mullins who
said that everyone had to go on working as if nothing
had happened. Despite this, almost everybody in
racing was harbouring serious doubts about it
continuing.

When F&M spread to Northern Ireland and then into the Cooley Peninsula in Co. Louth, it was the final straw. Up until that point, Minister for Agriculture, Joe Walsh, stated that those wishing to go to Cheltenham were free to do so. However he advised that those travelling to England with horses should stay on over there until the disease abated.

In reality, nobody was ever going to do that. Even before he made those comments, the Irish racing fraternity had decided en masse to stay at home. As they did so, the Cheltenham officials were left with no alternative but to cancel the 2001 Festival.

That decision was taken on 6th March during the temporary ban. They quickly realised that a Cheltenham without the Irish would be like a World Cup without Brazil.

Ireland's decision was taken mainly in support of farmers. The Horseracing and Agricultural industries are closely linked. To go on racing while many farmers were suffering terrible losses would have been selfish and insensitive. In the said circumstances, to travel to Cheltenham in search of prize money and big gambles would have been seen as immoral.

2001 was not the first time F&M had forced a closure of racing. In the winter of 1968, many big meetings fell foul of the disease including the King George. Through that bleak winter, racing was off for almost three months - even though Ireland remained free of the epidemic.

In hindsight, Willie Mullins would probably have wished that racing had been called off until Christmas. For when Florida Pearl finally returned, he was very lacklustre. After racing finally resumed, his next race was the Powers Gold Label Tote Gold Cup at Fairyhouse in April.

The Punchestown Festival was forced to close as authorities were not happy with the track and renovations had to be carried out. Therefore its entire meeting was transferred to Fairyhouse.

In that race, Florida Pearl was beaten by 14/1 shot Moscow Express trained by Francis Crowley. Following the race, it was decided to put him away for the summer and bring him back in the winter.

The situation then went from bad to worse. Reports surfaced once again suggesting that Florida Pearl was not showing any fire or zest at home on the gallops.

His winter return was in the James Nicholson at Down Royal. The rumours seem to have had foundation as he could only manage a poor third behind Foxchapel King trained by Michael 'Mouse' Morris.

Admittedly, Foxchapel King was having the best year of his racing career. After finishing second in the Irish National when he led to the last, he would later go on to capture some very big prizes.

All of this was of no consolation to connections of Florida Pearl. Things were not to their liking and hard as Mullins tried, he just could not get to the bottom of the problem.

A pattern was emerging of a winning and scintillating performance followed on by one or two poor and puzzling performances. Poor may not be the right word in light of all the very attractive place money he was picking up. Yet he just wasn't running as those closest to him knew he could.

Come December and there was no improvement. So much so that on the eve of his next race, he was confirmed in the newspapers as a doubtful starter. At the eleventh hour, Willie Mullins decided to go for it - if only to confirm or deny his King George entry just over two weeks later.

On Sunday 9th December, Florida Pearl was one of only four runners in the John Durkan at revamped Punchestown. Although a poor turnout, the race was billed as a rematch between Florida Pearl and Native Upmanship who had beaten him narrowly the year before.

He was a very attractive 5/1 but those odds reflected his poor recent form. It was also because of a horse called Sackville. Francis Crowley's young novice had strung together some impressive wins including the Charlie Hall at Wetherby. So impressive were his wins that he had already been installed as favourite for the 2002 Gold Cup.

Sackville did show promise in the race but at the second last he was a beaten horse. Perhaps he had had one race too many. Whatever the reason, Florida Pearl cruised past him and again, like the previous year, the challenge was thrown down by Native Upmanship.

Another ding dong battle ensued and after both jumped the last well, they settled down for a neck and neck battle all the way up the finishing straight. Exactly the same as the year before, it was 'on the nod' as they flashed past the post. This time it was Florida Pearl who bravely gained the day. Sackville was a disappointing third while Rince Ri was last of the quartet after an error strewn round.

Taking into account everything that had gone on before, it was an impressive display. The King George on St. Stephens Day was now confirmed as his next target.

There were several reasons in hoping for a good run in that race. At last he showed that he was back in good heart. The battling short head win at Punchestown was evidence in support of that. He had the experience of Kempton when second the year before. If he could remain in good form for a fortnight, the Mullins camp were hopeful, rather than confident, of a big run.

During a sobering and split second quiet moment, Willie Mullins heart sank. After all of his hard work in getting Florida Pearl back on track for Kempton, his hopes and optimism were dealt a jolt.

He had just finished talking to two of Ireland's top jockeys and a harsh realism set in. Ruby Walsh and Paul Carberry, both fit again after injury, were non-committal about riding Florida Pearl at Kempton.

Effectively, both apologised but stated that they were better off at home at Leopardstown's Christmas meeting. It wasn't that Florida Pearl could not win the King George. It was more a case of picking up a lot of lucrative big race rides rather than travelling to England for just the one. In their eyes it wasn't worth the risk. It was a big gamble they were not willing to take.

Receiving such news before was bad, but to get it again and from two top jockeys was a real blow to the solar plexus. With very little time at hand, a top jockey had to be found.

It would prove no easy task. Every avenue Mullins approached, he had to turn back. The usual candidates were either riding in the King George as well or they too had bookings elsewhere in Britain and Ireland.

After all the searching and lobbying, Archie O'Leary and Mullins decided to give the ride to JP McNamara. Although not an experienced jockey in big races, he was nonetheless young and talented and he was beginning to make a name for himself. Thrilled at getting the ride, the day before the race he was quoted as saying:

"It's unbelievable. Just to have my name next to the horse has made my Christmas".

On the morning of the race, Wetherby was abandoned. It was soon followed by the cancellation of Market Rasen. This alerted Mullins to the possibility of getting a top rider. McNamara was really a provisional booking and he had been told this and agreed to stand aside should another jockey become available.

Adrian Maguire was due to ride up north at Wetherby. When it was postponed he made his way to Market Rasen from his Oxfordshire home. When it too was abandoned he was in 'Nomans Land' in Leicester when Willie Mullins rang him on his mobile.

Maguire didn't hesitate in agreeing to take the ride. But he did warn the trainer that as he was only in the city of Leicester, he might not make it there on time. As the call ended, Maguire instructed his friend and driver, Andrew Lejeune, to turn around and head back south to Kempton. Going at full throttle to London, they soon encountered traffic congestion on the M25. At 12noon, it looked highly unlikely that they would make the race time of 2.20pm.

Eventually the traffic cleared and it paved the way for a smooth and fast passage to the Surrey venue just a few miles south of London. They arrived with a fair bit of time to spare - it was just after 1pm. As he prepared to mount up in the parade ring, Maguire was told to make the running if he so felt. Everything was now in his hands.

It was the very first time Adrian Maguire sat on the back of Florida Pearl but Willie Mullins knew he had a good man on board. Maguire won the race on Barton Bank in 1993 and he was cruelly denied a repeat the following year. Over 10lengths clear coming to the last, the horse unseated him. It was one of the most dramatic as well as heartbreaking last fence falls ever seen in racing.

First Gold was the one they all had to beat. As an impressive 10length winner the year before, he was the 6/4favourite. Florida Pearl saw a little money in the ring and went off at 8/1. In all, eight runners went to post. Bacchanal and Jonjo O'Neills Legal Right were also quietly fancied but the one dark horse they were all watching was Best Mate.

Henrietta Knight was telling anyone who cared to listen that her horse was the best she ever had and that he was a future star. The youngest horse in the race was also the mount of the mighty Tony McCoy. McCoy even went so far as to say that Best Mate was:
" potentially the best young chaser in Britain".

23,000 people turned up to watch a race full of intrigue. Millions more were watching on television. They were all to witness a fascinating race. It really began in earnest with Florida Pearl nipping up the inside rail and turning the screw with a full circuit still to go.

He was bowling along at the head of the field seemingly loving every minute of it. His jumping was foot perfect and at speed. He also relished the good ground conditions. In contrast, First Gold and Thierry Doumen were very uncomfortable with the move Maguire was making. It was a sucker punch and it was soon clear that he had nothing left in the tank to counter it. The belt had been relinquished.

Four fences from home and only four were left to fight it out for the King George crown. A mistake at the third last finally put the French bid to the sword. As First Gold gave way, three remained. The galloping Irish major was still in front and showing no signs of stopping.

All the time though, the young pretender Best Mate was going ominously well in behind. McCoy had yet to ask him any serious question. The brave Bacchanal finally gave way but only in the home straight. Up until then he looked a real serious threat but he could not quicken off the furious pace.

Sweeping down to the last and Florida Pearl was still in front. At a phenomenally high cruising speed, and from so far out, he was making a real bold bid. Master McCoy then swooped to deliver his challenge on the outside on Best Mate. It looked like they had judged the race and the pace perfectly. It was now just a matter of thrusting forward the final blow.

Florida Pearl took the last obstacle fast and fluently. His ears pricked back and his mouth open showing his yellowy brown teeth. If ever you saw a human like grimace and a look of determination on any animal, it was there - written on the face of a horse at war. For at his girth, just half a length behind and halfway across the fence, was an equally gritty Best Mate. His neck outstretched, he was ready for the fight - and a fight to the death it turned out to be.

Maguire swaying back and ready for the landing, McCoy crouching forward and pushing forth his partner for the attack. That photograph by Hugh Routledge, shown in colour in The Times (and produced on the front cover of this book) is arguably the finest expression of a final fence encounter between two top class horses.

Observing it over and over again, one gets the impression that the pause button has been pressed down. Press it again to release and they're over the last - heavy, hoarsey breathing sounds and the birch flying and flicking back like the sound of a sudden torrential shower pelting the pavement.

Both horses settled down to race at full speed on what they had left. It is probably no exaggeration to suggest that every man, woman and child watching, fully expected McCoy and Best Mate to swoop and conquer. After such a distance, and in the majority of cases, the horse coming from behind usually wins.

All the way up the Kempton run-in, as punishing in its own right as Cheltenhams hill, both combinations gave every ounce. Maguire in the Cork colours pushed,heaved and kicked.

In the twilight of his career, and with over a thousand winners behind him, in his eyes this finish could have been his final moment of glory. As such he rode like the devil and that fearless kid we remembered from years past. His style and his will rolled back those years and once again we were watching him on Cool Ground again - only this time he was in the front line. We were waiting for them to ultimately wilt.

In the Aston Villa colours of claret and blue, the real McCoy was at it again. A younger and very gifted horse guided by a younger and greatest ever jockey. He was coming to claim the race in that all too familiar style - crouching, kicking, pushing and whipping. Very few can withstand that ferocious assault. Very few can even hope to come out on top.

We waited and waited and waited. The gap was half a length but then closed to a neck. There was still fifty yards to go but the moment had come. McCoy was beginning to assert his authority aided by a very willing and talented horse.

It was a thriller and then, in a sudden moment, allegiances were switched. If any horse was deserving of such a prize, it was Florida Pearl. So near so many times and so near now. The line was tantalisingly close. Come on Florida, come on, come on!

As victory loomed large in the eyes of McCoy, Maguire and the Pearl shut it firmly. They went on again as the winning post neared and at the line they had three parts of a length to spare. A truly magnificent joust had been settled. To the victor the spoils and after travelling up M1s and down M25s to Kemptons finishing straight, the job had been completed.

Two class horses and jockeys fought out a tight finish that began halfway across the last and was only settled a few yards from the line. It will live long in the memory of National Hunt enthusiasts and when they come to replay that finish over and over again, they may as well start it rolling just before take-off at the final fence. Otherwise, the essence of what was a gripping encounter will be lost.

The quality and greatness of the race was also echoed in some post race statistics. Florida was the first Irish horse in 26 years to win the King George after the great Captain Christy in 1975. The winning time of 5mins 57.95secs was just outside the standard of 5mins 55secs. First Gold's winning time the year before, albeit in good to soft ground, was 5.59.8secs. To illustrate just how fast Kempton is, Florida's two winning times in the previous two Hennesseys, even allowing for softish ground, were 6.59.9 and 6.28.4 respectively.

Obviously delighted after the race, almost everyone had something to say. Willie Mullins immediately nominated a third tilt at the Gold Cup as the obvious target. He also had a swipe at all the horse's critics when he said:

"It really doesn't bother me what they say about him. He is the best I've ever trained and probably the best I will ever have. His jumping has improved and he seems bigger and stronger than ever".

Adrian Maguire talked to reporters more about his escapades along the motorways than the race itself! He was nevertheless delighted to have won the race for a second time and erase the painful memories of Barton Bank in 1994. In stark contrast, JP McNamara said: "I knew Adrian was coming down but Ruby Walsh and Paul Carberry missed out too.
It was a great honour just to have my name next to Florida Pearl. I am gutted to lose out though. I am human".

One of Florida's biggest admirers over the years has been Alastair Down of the Racing Post and Channel 4 Racing. In his column next day, he wrote:

"You wouldn't mind owning a 'nearly horse' with nearly £725,000 in prize money nestling under the mattress".

In a similar tone, Archie O'Leary said:
"Some of the local papers described him as too old. If that's what age does, then I'm happy".

Very sportingly, Best Mate's trainer Henrietta Knight had her own very kind words of praise. After coming so close to winning, she said very graciously:

"I'm delighted for Florida Pearl and for Willie - they have been the runner-up so many times. They deserved to win a big race like this. I had a couple of pounds on him too!".

Florida Pearl had just etched himself into a little bit of history and immortality. When his obituary is written, forget the number of wins or the amount of money won. Instead, just carve out the following words:

FLORIDA PEARL. ONE OF ONLY 4 IRISH HORSES TO HAVE WON THE KING GEORGE FOLLOWING THE GREAT ARKLE, COTTAGE RAKE AND CAPTAIN CHRISTY

CHAPTER 8

ONE IN A MILLION

That thrilling King George win was without question, the highlight of Florida's career up to this point. When all the celebrations and back-slapping died down, the Hennessey was now very much the focus and an attempt to win it for a record fourth time. But having scaled the heights of Kempton, the months of February and March 2002 would bring everyone right back down to earth.

Only five runners went to post for the Hennessey and that only served to make Florida's poor run even more disappointing. He trailed home over 25lengths fourth behind the winner, his stable companion Alexander Banquet. The heavy ground did not help matters but perhaps the win over Best Mate had taken more out of him than expected. Things were about to get a lot worse.

In his third attempt at winning the Gold Cup at
Cheltenham, Florida hit rock bottom. He could only
manage 11th of the 13 finishers and it was the worst run
of his life. Boat Mate, whom he had beaten at Kempton,
gained his revenge in what was to be the first of his
three-in-a-row Gold Cups. Florida beat him by three
quarters of a length previously but this time he was 40
lengths in arrears.

It subsequently transpired that Florida had been
suffering from a respiratory infection. After a little rest
to allow the ailment to clear, Aintree's Grand National
meeting in April was now given the thumbs up.
Although Florida was allotted top weight of 11st 10lbs
for the National, Mullins opted to go for the Martell
Cup instead.

Adrian Maguire picked up a bad injury prior to
Cheltenham. It was an injury so bad that it would
eventually spell the end of his great career. Conor
O'Dwyer replaced Adrian at Cheltenham and Barry
Geraghty then became the eight jockey to partner
Florida when they teamed up in the Martell Cup.

Two days before that race, Tony McCoy entered
racing's record books for the umpteenth time. He won
on Valiramix at Warwick and it was his 270th winner of
the season! It broke his own record but it also shattered
the 55 year old record set by Sir Gordon Richards for
the number of winners in a season. Up until that day, the
2nd April 2002, many felt that original record would
never be beaten.

With the sun on his back, Florida enjoyed every minute of his Martell Cup run. In the race he never had a moments worry. Geraghty settled him early and then the pair took up the running seven fences out. They won eased down by 11lengths from the McCoy ridden Cyfor Malta. Lord Noelie, who burst a blood vessel during the race, finished a further neck behind in third.

Willie Mullins had some explaining to do after the race. With regard to Florida, for the first time the stewards called him in to account for the great improvement in his form. He explained about the respiratory infection and as a result, the stewards decided to take no action. However they did order that the horse be routinely tested.

Florida was back in winning form again and Mullins was very pleased and as much relieved as anything else. He told the media afterwards:

"He had a bit of an infection after Cheltenham and I had to treat him with antibiotics.
I would love to get him to Cheltenham in the form he was in today. He was never 100pc for his three Gold Cup runs. Now he will head to Punchestown for the Heineken Chase which to date has not been a lucky race for him".

On this occasion, it proved to be a happy hunting ground. Geraghty kept the ride for that race on April 24th and they won by 3lengths. Though the manner of his win was far from comfortable. At the fourth last, Florida made an horrendous mistake. He showed great courage and determination to go on and win as several others looked to be going better at the time.

Conor o'Dwyer on the runner up Native Upmanship felt a little hard done. He said:

"I got hassle from Foxchapel King who was making mistakes and Sackville who was jumping to the left. I'm not saying that it cost me the race but it didn't help".

Sackville, a bright and shining star at the start of his career, was now becoming a fading light. He took a crashing fall at the last when beaten. Incidentally, his jockey John Cullen received a one day ban for excessive use of the whip prior to the fall.

On Monday 20th May, Florida Pearl was officially confirmed as the best 3mile chaser in Britain and Ireland. At the National Hunt Classifications held in the Stand House Hotel in The Curragh, he was rated one pound superior to Best Mate. That was despite the fact the English horse trounced him in the Gold Cup!

British Horseracing Board handicapper, Phil Smith explained the reason for that rating:

"We believe that the best performance of the season was by Florida Pearl in the King George VI Chase. He won three other Graded races and at their best he comes out above Best Mate".

His Irish counterpart, Noel O'Brien, raised doubts about the merit of Best Mate's Gold Cup win when he added: "It looked like the best race of the season on the ratings, but the running of Commanche Court(second) and See More Business(third) at the age of 12 raised doubts".

Florida was put out to grass for the summer. One of his targets when coming back for the 2002/03 season was the Grand National. A statement which Willie Mullins made after the Heineken win was probably the key to what would turn out to be a really miserable year. He stated that the mistake at the fourth last was the worst of his career and he went on:

"Even when he fell at Leopardstown a few years ago, he didn't get it as wrong as he did at that fence".

In early November 2002, Florida lined up for the James
Nicholson at Down Royal. It would be the beginning of
a season to forget. On soft going, he could only manage
fourth of the seven runners. A lifeless and very
disappointing performance saw him finish almost 23
lengths behind the 14/1 winner, More Than A Stroll
trained by Arthur Moore.

Those close to the horse were baffled. It was hard to
stomach, but after digesting it, the poor run was put
down to the ground conditions allied to his first run
after the summer. No such excuses could be blamed for
his next race where once more he flopped badly.
Returning to Kempton to defend his King George
crown, this time Best Mate turned the tables. In the field
of ten, Florida was fourth under Ruby Walsh.

Fourth in such a prestigious race was no mean feat. In
truth though, he was beaten 18lengths and only really
ran on past beaten and tired horses.

Nevertheless, far from showing any displeasure or
despondency, Willie Mullins saw some encouraging
signs. He said:

"He was there to the fourth last and I'm certainly not
unhappy. We'll have to plan where he runs next but he
seems to have come out of the race well enough and
certainly wasn't distressed or anything".

Following his next run, suspicions and doubts about Florida's well-being came very much to the fore. Bidding to win the 2003 Hennessey for the fourth time, he was pulled up in a small field of five. Beef or Salmon trained by Michael Hourigan was an impressive 5length winner. It was the first time Florida had failed to finish a race bar falling.

The ground was 'yielding to soft' and so this time there were definitely no excuses. Though not showing it, those in the Mullins camp were bewildered by these runs. They could not find any answers and they just had to soldier on and hope for improvement.

Florida Pearl arrived at the 2003 Cheltenham Festival in the poorest form of his career. This time the Gold Cup was swerved in favour of the Queen Mother Champion Chase. The Gold Cup decision was a wise one as Best Mate won it for the second year running.

The Queen Mother race proved to be another disaster in a never-ending season of woe. Florida, at a biggest ever price of 12/1, was run off his feet by the speedy 2milers. Ireland won the race with Jessica Harrington's Moscow Flyer. Beaten 34lengths, Florida looked a sad sight as he trailed in last of the eight finishers.

In hindsight, it was a mistake to bend to media pressure and run Florida in such a fast race against younger and speedier opponents. Perhaps that 2mile option should have been taken years earlier. Moscow Flyer was always going to prove a very tough nut to crack.

Charlie Swan, former Irish champion jockey, said on the eve of that race:
"Moscow Flyer was the only horse who scared me when Istabraq was around and he has shown just how brilliant he is over fences".

The O'Leary's and all in the Willie Mullins yard were obviously going through torment. No concrete answers could explain his huge dip in form. They could only march on and hope that the horse could redeem himself in his final race of the season. During the summer months, they could then try and get to the bottom of the problem.

On the last day of April, he ran in the Heineken at Punchestown. It did not augur well when he was sent off at odds of 9/1 in the small field. A great price for a horse with undoubted class and ability. But on current form it would have taken a very brave punter to go in with big money down.

There was to be no end in sight for the misery. Florida could only manage to finish fifth of the seven runners. It was a very bad end to a very bad year - the worst in his eight year career. Never before had Florida failed to deliver a big prize in a season.

There must have been a problem and it had to be sorted out quickly. An empty season and form figures of '44P85' were too bad to be true.

Archie O'Leary sat down with Willie Mullins prior to the 2003/04 season. They put their heads together in an effort to find the root cause of Florida's failings. It was not just a case of his failure to win a race that was bothering both men. The sparkle that had so often lit up the Pearl, was no longer glistening as it should.

His age of 11, going on 12, was not seen as the problem. Plenty of horses win races aged 13. Besides, Florida always had a zest for life and for racing and this was very noticeable by its absence. Trawling back over his races, they did begin to see a pattern which had emerged over the years. It was just a hunch but perhaps somewhere within that pattern lay the reason for the horse's lacklustre performances.

When Florida won his first five races in a row, he looked unbeatable. Then he took a very heavy fall at Leopardstown and after that, he was never quite the same. A winning run was generally followed by at least one but sometimes two inept displays. Willie had a feeling that in that fall, he may have suffered an injury to his back.

It was never properly investigated for several reasons. On the outside, there were no obvious injuries and in the middle of a busy racing season, there were other priorities. Then, in between a poor run when Florida would come back to winning ways, the whole thing would be put on the back boiler and forgotten about.

During the summer of 2001, a possible reason was finally found. Willie Mullin's head girl, Tracey Gilmour, found a lump on Florida's right hind leg. X-rays revealed that the 'splint-bone' had a double fracture. Although it was only a minor bone, it must have caused some degree of discomfort.

After a couple of months rest, he was nursed back to full health by Tracey. The patient must have been very grateful as he went on to land the King George just a very short time after that. Commenting on that injury, Tracey said:

"He was sore in his back just under one side of the saddle. Very often if one part of the body is injured, another will compensate for it and then that part too will become overused and hurt. Maybe he had a fracture on that splint-bone for some time. We knew he was not quite sound but we never knew where the problem was".

That was 2001 so, following the debacle of the 2002/03 season, maybe the injury had surfaced once more. There was also the possibility that another unexplored injury was lying undiscovered somewhere in his body. Going back to the Heineken at the end of the 2001/02 season, Willie Mullins was on record as saying that the error at the fourth last, "was the worst blunder of his career". He also said it was worse than his fall at Leopardstown. Had this Punchestown blunder caused another injury or could it even have exacerbated the older injury. Mullins felt he had to check it out. The vets could not find anything amiss so he decided to turn to someone more unorthodox.

Grainne ni Chaba had a great feeling and understanding for horses. Some likened her approach to that of a 'horse whisperer' similar to that of the character played by Robert Redford in the 1998 film of the same name.

Grainne shuns the term referring instead to her 25 years experience of working with and getting to know horses. She runs the Curragh Animal Physiotherapy clinic in Kildare. She is also the only Irish equine therapist with International Association of Horse Therapist qualifications.

In an interview given to Ronnie Bellew of the Sunday Independent, she explained some of her work and what she tries to do:
"You have to learn how to read a horses mind and interpret the signals they are giving off when you are treating them. How they are feeling is all there in the eyes, the nose, the twitching of the ears, the way they lick and chew. The horse has to be able to get a certain feeling from me and I have to be able to feel what the horse is telling me".

As a result of her work with Florida, Grainne felt in no doubt that there was something amiss. In her opinion, the horse was more mentally fatigued than anything else. She did tend to his old injured spots and she did various stretching exercises with him. However, her diagnosis was that Florida had become a bit of a lone soldier rather than a battle-weary warhorse. In short, he was a little depressed and lonely.

Just like the old proverb, 'All work and no play....', Grainne felt that Florida needed a little stimulation by having some much-needed company. So she arranged for Florida to meet some new equine friends. As she recalled:
"I have a little jumper here called Chubaka. I put Florida in the same barn with him and other horses where they could touch and talk to each other. It was like a retreat or holiday for him. The contact with Chubaka and the other horses seemed to give him a new lease of life".

After his extended holiday, Florida made his belated 2003/04 racecourse reappearance on 13th January 2004. The race was the Normans Grove Chase at Fairyhouse. Now just turned 12, the race was seen as a gentle comeback and a chance to blow off the cobwebs.

Richard Johnson resumed his partnership and while they were expected to win this race which was upped to Grade 3 status, getting him race fit was the main purpose.

All of Grainne's work came to fruition as Florida made the perfect return. He won the race by 2lengths after taking up the running after the third fence. From there to the winning post he was engaged in a real gunfight with old rival, Rince Ri. Apart from a slight mistake at the fourth last, he never touched a twig.

Although not overly impressive, William Hill did make Florida 12/1 favourite for the Grand National after that run. His next intended run at Ascot was shelved due to bad weather and so it was on to Leopardstown for the perennial Hennessey.

In that race on February 8th, he would be bidding to win it for a record 4th time.

18,000 people attended the Leopardstown feature on what was a glorious day for that time of year. The warm sunny day meant that the ground was perfect and because of that, punters saw some value in Florida's price. A few days before the race he was available at 10/1 but on the day, his price was cut to 5/1.

The 7 year-old Cloudy Bays, the youngest in the field, set out to make the running. He clouted several fences and the six behind had to tread carefully as a result. By the time the field came to the fourth last, he was a spent force. Florida was thoroughly enjoying himself as he lobbed along under Johnson. At the fourth last they went to the front. All of a sudden they had all bar Harbour Pilot in big trouble.

Clearing the third last, the race was between the two. But as they ran to the second last, Richard Johnson was just working that little bit harder on Florida. Paul Carberry hadn't moved a muscle on Harbour Pilot. He was going very well but there was still a long way to go and two fences remaining.

Awwww! An almighty gasp bellowed from the crowd as Harbour Pilot came crashing down. Paul Carberry had no chance as the horse failed to lift off. They just crashed through the fence and Carberry was ejected from the saddle.

Suddenly, an unbelievable scenario was unfolding before the eyes of thousands viewing the race. Florida was out on his own in front. Could he make it home and into the history books forever.

After all the past glories and the doom and gloom of the previous season, he was now so close to an even greater achievement. Real racing folk and the romantics were willing him on. Willie Mullins, Archie and Violet, Tracey Gilmour and almost everybody were wide eyed and holding their breath. Everything was happening so quickly. One moment Harbour Pilot was coming to claim the race, and the next Florida was left all alone in front.

Nervous moments still lay ahead. As he came to the last, it was evident that his stride was slowing. In behind, Rince Ri and Le Coudray were making ground. Legs that had leapt some of the toughest fences around - Cheltenham, Aintree, Kempton, Punchestown - were now required to pop just one more fence. In his 33 race career, he may not have had much mileage on the clock, but he had plenty of wear and tear.

Hallelujah and Jaysus, Mary and sweet Joseph and every expletive you can imagine was spewed out as the loose Harbour Pilot cut across Florida just as he was about to take the last! Richard Johnson's face etched alarm and sudden shock. He gave Florida a quick tug and it was just enough to avoid a collision or a 'carried-out'. As the loose horse in front jumped diagonally across him, its tail wiped Florida's nose - and the beads of cold sweat on Johnson's face!

In behind, Le Coudray was bursting forth and past
Rince Ri. On the run-in, Florida began to slow and he
was running up and down on the same spot. Le Coudray
was closing fast. The drama continued. It still wasn't
over and everyone was calling the fat lady to sing. The
intensity was akin to a hurling encounter at level scores
entering the final minute.

Johnson pushed and pushed and kicked and kicked. As
they entered the final fifty yards, only then it became
apparent that Le Coudray had no more to give. Florida
won by 3lengths. Emotions were then let loose at last.
There were whoops of delight amid the screams and the
cheers. Of course there were also plenty of tears.

All of this in the winners enclosure that he was entering
for a record-breaking fourth time. Florida had beaten
the great Jodami's record of three wins in the
Hennessey. It was an amazing feat and one which will
take a long time to beat or equal, if ever. The
newspaper hacks clambered for words to fill their pages
next morning. They were given plenty to write by the
joyful connections. None more so than an ecstatic
Willie Mullins who declared:

"I enjoyed that more than any other race I have ever
won. I think that was as good a performance as he has
ever given. This is a remarkable horse, he is so sound. It
will be straight to the Gold Cup with him now".

Willie could be forgiven for perhaps going a little overboard with that statement. It was understandable in the circumstances. Let us not forget another milestone that Florida achieved that day. The first prize of E95,000 pushed his career earnings through the one million euro barrier. Not bad for an initial outlay of £50,000. As Willie so rightfully said, a remarkable horse. A horse that only comes along every twenty years or so. An outstanding horse and certainly one in a million.

Credit for nurturing such an Irish gem

Kate Austin says it's great Florida Pearl can now enjoy retirement after a consistent career at the top

ALASTAIR DOWN'S appreciation of Florida Pearl was spot on (*July 30*).

His King George win was one of the best exhibitions of fluency and fearlessness that I have ever seen. All connections deserve the utmost credit for the way they nurtured this Irish gem, while never shirking the challenges he was set by young pretenders.

Florida Pearl will be missed by all jumping fans, but isn't it great that he has survived the rigours of a consistently high-level jumps career to now enjoy a happy retirement?

KATE AUSTIN
Leyton

FOND FAREWELL FLORIDA

On 3rd March 2004, Willie Mullins announced that Florida Pearl would miss the Cheltenham Gold Cup through injury. He had picked up a ligament injury and it was now highly unlikely that he would ever race again.

Although the injury eventually healed, his very caring owners decided to call it a day. At the Galway Races on Ladies Day, Thursday 29th July, Florida was officially retired. Among all the beautiful people present, he was paraded around the paddock before racing began. Beside him were his loyal and loving handler, Tracey Gilmour and the man who partnered him in his greatest triumph, Adrian Maguire.

Throughout his magnificent career, praise and popularity were very shortcoming. But on his retirement day, RTE Racing presenters Ted Walsh and Robert Hall paid very generous tributes.

The following day, the Racing Post with its front page headline and double page insert, led the newspaper brigade. However, some of the bigger newspapers should have been ashamed for their glaring omissions.

Without any shadow of doubt, Florida was Ireland's greatest modern day chaser. Trawl through the records of the others, and it will become quite clear that Florida's record here, and especially in England, will be very hard to match. Not since the days of Arkle and Captain Christy have we ever seen his like - as a mare, Dawn Run was the best of her sex but even her record is arguably not as impressive as Florida's.

Performing at the highest level for an incredible seven years, he won 16 of his 33 races. He only finished out of the frame on nine occasions and five of those were in the miserable 2002/03 season when the end was in sight.

The very highly respected publication Timeform, recognised as the 'bible' of racing, acknowledged this. They stated that Florida has to be among the Top 6 Irish Chasers of, quote:

"the last 30 years or so and in terms of showing top class form over a sustained period, he is almost out on his own".

Just why Florida failed to attract an adoring public still remains a mystery. The Racing Post's eminent writer, Alastair Down, was forever seeking an answer to that poser in his writings about Florida. A public that embraced so lovingly the likes of Danoli, Dorans Pride, Desert Orchid, One Man and See More Business ignored Florida en masse.

Florida Pearl was an ugly brute. There is no question about that. The handsome physical features present in a horse like Best Mate were absent in Florida. Standing seventeen hands high, Florida had a rather big white patch running down the length of his large boney head.

His body was also a mass of muscle and it all added up to making him look more like a farm workhorse than a classy racehorse. But therein the mystery deepens further as very often such features can touch a soft spot in a lot of people.

That he failed to win a Gold Cup cannot be the reason. Danoli and Dorans Pride also failed in that department yet they were more popular. Imperial Call won a Gold Cup and was not as popular as the aforementioned. Perhaps if we now turned the clock back, he would finally win the 'top of the pops' hands down.

Those magic memories which he created will live long in the memory. As a baby, he drove the crowds at Cheltenham wild with delight. The banker swept round the final bend in the hands of Dunwoody to win easily. A year later, as a novice chaser, he banked the money again in the Sun Alliance.

As a man he came of age with many Grade 1 wins at Leopardstown, Punchestown, Aintree, Down Royal and Fairyhouse. His finest moment will forever go down as one of those greatest ever finishes. In beating the great Best Mate ridden by the great Tony McCoy, he fought out one of the all time great tussles - a real duel.

An old veteran, in the twilight of his career, he had even more to give. It is entirely appropriate that in his final two races, in his final season, he won them both. So many in sport strive to go out at the top or on a winning note. To do that and to create records in the process was a very fitting end to an already hugely successful career.

Florida flew the Irish flag and he done this nation proud. On a good day, and running in full health, he may well have went one better and landed a Gold Cup. It matters not. In many great careers there is always and inevitably one piece missing. Florida stayed every yard of the trip. In doing so, he gave us all many minutes and hours, months and years of fun and distance run.

In retirement, we wish him well. May he continue to enjoy the company of other horses and although he will no doubt miss the racetrack, hopefully he will dream all those great days again. Somehow, racing and Leopardstown will not be the same without him.

So thanks for those fantastic moments Florida. Thanks also to Archie and Violet, Willie and Tracey, his work riders, his jockeys, his carers - he has come home safely. You all helped to create a legend and as each year of the Hennessey goes by, his record will be mentioned. Until it is broken, if ever, his legacy will live on for decades to come.

FLORIDA PEARL STATISTICS

OVERALL RECORD OF RACES

SEASON	RUNS	1st	2nd	3rd	4th	Unpl	Fell	P/Up	%
*1995-96	1	1	-	-	-	-	-	-	100
1996-97	2	2	-	-	-	-	-	-	100
1997-98	3	3	-	-	-	-	-	-	100
1998-99	4	1	1	1	-	-	1	-	25
1999-00	5	3	2	-	-	-	-	-	60
2000-01	5	1	3	-	1	-	-	-	20
2001-02	7	4	-	1	1	1	-	-	57
2002-03	5	-	-	-	2	2	-	1	0
2003-04	2	2	-	-	-	-	-	-	100
TOTAL	34	17	6	2	4	3	1	1	50

RECORD OF DISTANCES RUN

MILES	FURLONGS	RUNS	WINS	%
2	-	1	1	100
2	1	2	2	100
2	2	-	-	-
2	3	2	2	100
2	4	2	1	50
2	5	1	1	100
2	6	-	-	-
2	7	-	-	-
3	-	*16	*6	37
3	1	7	4	57
3	2	3	0	0

OFFICIAL GOING RECORD

GOING	WINS
FIRM	0
GOOD TO FIRM	1
GOOD	* 5
YIELDING	3
GOOD TO SOFT	0
YIELDING TO SOFT	2
SOFT	4
HEAVY	2

RECORD OF JOCKEYS

NAME	RIDES	WINS	%	GRADE 1s
* Mr. A G Costello	1	1	100	0
Mr. J A Nash	1	1	100	0
Richard Dunwoody	8	5	62	3
Paul Carberry	8	4	50 **	3
Ruby Walsh	4	0	0	0
Richard Johnson	4	3	75	2
Adrian Maguire	2	1	50	1
Conor O'Dwyer	1	0	0	0
Barry Geraghty	5	2	40	1

* Point to Point race before official career under Rules of Racing

** James Nicholson Chase at Down Royal was upped to Grade 1
3 years later

RECORD OF GRADE 1 WINS

DATE	RACECOURSE	RACE
12th March 1997	Cheltenham	Champion Bumper
18th March 1998	Cheltenham	Sun Alliance Novice Chase
7th Feb 1999	Leopardstown	Hennessey Gold Cup
6th Nov 1999	Down Royal	James Nicholson Chase
6th Feb 2000	Leopardstown	Hennessey Gold Cup
4th Feb 2001	Leopardstown	Hennessey Gold Cup
9th Dec 2001	Punchestown	John Durkan Chase
26th Dec 2001	Kempton Park	King George V1 Chase
24th Mar 2002	Punchestown	Heineken Gold Cup
8th Feb 2004	Leopardstown	Hennessey Gold Cup

FLORIDA PEARL FACTS

BIGGEST WIN MARGIN:
20length defeat of Delphi Lodge, 26/12/1997

BIGGEST WIN MARGIN IN GRADE 1:
11length defeat of Cyfor Malta, 4/4/2002

SHORTEST WIN MARGIN:
Short Head defeat of Amberleigh House, 23/1/2000

SHORTEST WIN MARGIN GRADE 1:
Short Head defeat of Native Upmanship, 9/12/01

BIGGEST S.P.:
12/1, Queen Mother Champion Chase, 12/3/03

SHORTEST S.P.:
2/5, BAX Handicap Chase, 23/1/00

BIGGEST WIN S.P. :
8/1, Normans Grove Chase, 18/1/04 8/1 King George V1 Chase, 26/12/01

BIGGEST FIELD:
Won 25 runner Champion Bumper, Cheltenham 1997

SMALLEST FIELD:
Won 4 runner BAX, Leopardstown 2000,
Won 4 runner John Durkan, Punchestown 2001

LONGEST UNBEATEN RUN:
5 races from 26/12/96 to 18/3/98

LONGEST LOSING RUN:
also 5 races from 9/11/02 to 30/4/03

RECORD OF FLORIDA'S MILLION

WIN PRIZEMONEY

Date	Course	Amount/Euro
26/12/1996	Leopardstown	5,218.60
12/03/1997	Cheltenham	24,060.90
29/12/1997	Leopardstown	5,218.60
08/02/1998	Leopardstown	41,266.50
18/03/1998	Cheltenham	80,004.40
07/02/1999	Leopardstown	77,454.00
06/11/1999	Down Royal	76,184.30
23/01/2000	Leopardstown	12,379.90
06/02/2000	Leopardstown	83,104.40
04/02/2001	Leopardstown	87,294.50
09/12/2001	Punchestown	57,773.10
26/12/2001	Kempton	136,379.30
04/04/2002	Aintree	114,098.40
24/04/2002	Punchestown	99,600.00
18/01/2004	Fairyhouse	20,800.00
08/02/2004	Leopardstown	97,700.00
TOTAL WIN MONEY		**1,018,536.90**

PLACE PRIZE MONEY

Date	Course	Position	Amount/Euro
18/03/1999	Cheltenham	3rd	39,090.80
28/04/1999	Punchestown	2nd	30,473.70
28/12/1999	Leopardstown	2nd	19,046.10
16/03/2000	Cheltenham	2nd	97,769.80
18/11/2000	Down Royal	4th	5,586.80
10/12/2000	Punchestown	2nd	12,697.40
26/12/2000	Kempton	2nd	52,376.70
25/04/2001	Fairyhouse	2nd	31,743.40
10/11/2001	Down Royal	3rd	13,967.40
10/02/2002	Leopardstown	4th	6,400.00
09/11/2002	Down Royal	4th	5,600.00
26/12/2002	Kempton	4th	15,611.50
30/04/2003	Punchestown	5th	3,200.00

TOTAL PLACE MONEY   333,563.60

TOTAL PRIZE MONEY   1,352,100.50

FLORIDA PEARL RECORDS & ACHIEVEMENTS

4 HENNESSEY GOLD CUPS

In winning the Irish Hennessey Gold Cup at
Leopardstown in 1999, 2000, 2001 and 2004, Florida
Pearl broke the record of the great English horse Jodami
who won it 3 times.

A very proud record and one which will take some
beating - and indeed equalling.

Florida Pearl's 3 in a row from 1999-2001 also equalled
Jodami's 3 in a row, 1993-1995.

GRADE 1 CHELTENHAM DOUBLE

Florida Pearl became the first and so far only horse to
have completed, in back to back years, the Grade 1
double of Champion Bumper and Champion Novices
Chase (Sun Alliance), 1997 and 1998.

KING GEORGE VI CHASE

Florida Pearl is the first Irish horse in modern times to have won Kempton's Christmas showpiece. Following on from the great Arkle, he is also only the fourth Irish horse to have won it since the race began.

BEATEN BEST MATE

Florida Pearl is the only Irish trained horse to have beaten triple Gold Cup winner Best Mate over fences.

MILLIONAIRE'S CLUB

In amassing over a million euro in prize money, Florida Pearl has also entered Irish Sport's Millionaires Club. He has also joined just a handful of jumpers in the club - most notably Istabraq, Moscow Flyer and Dorans Pride.

ALL – TIME TOP 100

In a well publicised and extensive poll carried out by the Racing Post in 2003, Florida Pearl numbered 34 in the "Top 100 of the Most Popular Race Horses Of All Time". Arkle topped the pole with Red Rum just behind. Interestingly, Best Mate poled in the mid twenties.